SAYING IT WITH

Flowers

SAYING IT WITH

Flowers

THE STORY OF THE FLOWER SHOP

JENNIFER DAVIES

HEADLINE

First published in 2000
by HEADLINE BOOK PUBLISHING

10 9 8 7 6 5 4 3 2 1

British Library Cataloguing in Publication Data
Davies, Jennifer
Saying it with flowers
1. Florists – Great Britain – History
I Title
381.4'56359'0941
ISBN 0 7472 7405 3

Designed by Ellembee

Printed and bound in Italy by Canale & C.S.p.A.

HEADLINE BOOK PUBLISHING
A division of Hodder Headline
338 Euston Road, London NW1 3BH

www.headline.co.uk
www.hodderheadline.com

❧ Contents ❧

Acknowledgements

I sincerely thank the following kind individuals who have given up their time to talk to me and provide material in the way of stories, background information and photographs for this book: Timothy Barringer; Nancy Bealing; Raymond Bealing; Kathleen Bretherick; Janet and Peter Carter; Jonathan Case; John Collingridge; Joan Corles; Ron Cypher; Ken Davis; Elaine Dent; George Dudfield; Bob Fowler and Diana Fowler; Daphne Glyn of the Friends of St Mary's, Paddington; John Godsmark; Derek Goodyear; Lawson Gwillim; Melvin Hall; Rosanne Hall; Jill Harding; Jean Harrison; Jonathan Harrison; Jane and Brian Hawkins; Prue and Terry Headey; Christine Hinds; the Jefferies family; Penny Lewis; Sandy Lewis; Bill Lister; David Longman; Sheila Macqueen; Simon Marshall; Margaret Matheson; Derek Owen Morgan; the Nattress family; John Paynter; Jean Pinkham of the Edmonton Hundred Historical Society; Gordon Price; Edith Richardson; Ken Rigeon; Jim and Patrick Segar; Katherine Sloan; Gwen Stock; Waynman Strike; Mary Surrey; the Treseder family; Alice Wood; and Colin Woolley.

I would also like to thank the following organizations and bodies for their kind help: Ayscoughfee Hall Museum, South Holland District Council; Bath and North East Somerset Archives and Records Office; Birmingham Museum and Art Gallery; Dr Steven Blake, Keeper of Collections, Cheltenham Museum; Institute of Bookbinding and Allied Trades; the Special Collections Department at the Boole Library, University College, Cork; British Association Representing Breeders; Bromesberrow Place Nurseries; Cheltenham Reference Library; Constance Spry Flower School in Farnham; Dorchester Hotel; Museum of English Rural Life, University of Reading; Flowers and Plants Association; The Gilbert Library, Dublin; Hallmark Cards UK; Harrods Archives; Interflora, Florists Telegraph Delivery Association; the John Henry Company; Ledbury Library; Lincolnshire County Council (Local Studies Department); Newcastle Library (Local Studies Department); Protheroe, Carter and Eason; Royal Collection Enterprises Limited; the Lindley Library of the Royal Horticultural Society; Smithers-Oasis Company; Southampton City Heritage Services; the Savoy Group florists and the Savoy Group archivist, Susan Scott; St Clement Danes Church; Tullie House Museum and Art Gallery, Carlisle; Museum of Welsh Life, St Fagans, Cardiff; Welwyn Garden City Library (Local Studies section); and Widdups of Bradford.

I am indebted to Fiona and Robert Dean for providing location facilities for the photographs specially taken by Frank Tomlinson; and I thank Cinna Belloc Lowdes, Sarah Blizard, Jane Cadbury and Selina Marcon for supplying props and invaluable help.

Many people have contributed to this book and I am truly grateful to them. However, among the many, I would particularly like to thank: Robin Wayne for his kindness and all the archive florists' material both written and otherwise, which he has loaned; Joan Pearson who, from the time when this book was merely an idea, has given encouragement, stories and assistance; Bob Fowler for being a mentor and a fund of knowledge; and Lynda Owen who has not only designed and executed all the floral work for our specially commissioned photos but with characteristic kindness and cheerfulness has always been ready to help and advise.

Aside from my floristry friends the book would not have happened if Heather Holden-Brown, Non-fiction Publishing Director at Headline, had not commissioned and encouraged it and I thank her sincerely for doing both. Also at Headline, Jo Roberts-Miller has offered great editorial guidance overall and together with the editor, Anne Askwith, did much to help the structure and chronology of what at times must have seemed to them a rambling text. I thank them both. I am also grateful to Rachel Geere, Bryone Picton and Rebecca Purtell for the part they have played in bringing the book together and to notice.

Finally, I thank Linda Blakemore, a designer and a long-standing friend, for everything she has done towards this book and the support she has given throughout.

Truly, books are the work of many hands.

Jennifer Davies

Introduction

People are sometimes kind enough to ask me, 'What are you writing about?' and, while working on this book, I replied, 'Flower shops – from the times when they began.' Enquirers who liked flowers would say, 'Oh, that'll be interesting.' However, from those not so minded there'd be a look of faint desperation while they struggled to think of a polite comment on a subject that was as alien to them as, well, the Marble Arch traffic roundabout in London would be to my hens. In fact, one fellow said disbelievingly: 'Are there *enough* interesting things to be said about flower shops to fill a book?'

Oh, yes, and yes, and yes. Particularly when it is not me doing the telling but people for whom the business has been their lives – whether in florist's shops, flower markets or in growing flowers. For the most part this book is their words; I have just added historical detail and the background to how and why certain events occurred.

In this way, flowers have been – and I am sorry if this sounds a fanciful metaphor – a bunch of keys opening a variety of subjects. To mention but a few from around Britain: a Scot's florist recalls making a traditional mock wedding bouquet of vegetables which had been ordered by the workmates of an Aberdeen bride; Oxford florists explain how they carry on the old custom of supplying carnations of certain set colours to college students taking exams; and the last outpost of Sul y Blodau (Flowering Sunday) in Wales is apparently thriving west of Llanelli. In addition, flowers have been the 'keys' to learning stories about royal weddings, gypsy funerals, the first shipboard flower shop and a wartime horse and haycart flower-delivery trek of over seventy miles from West Sussex to London's Covent Garden.

As the experiences and memories of those who have kindly contributed to this book span many different subjects and also, particularly if their parents and grand-parents were florists, many years, the story that has emerged is not so much a strictly chronological one as a series of themes that collectively create a picture of the world of flower shops since they began.

Opposite: The Bunch of Lilacs *by James Jacques Joseph. Decorating the home with plants and cut flowers became very fashionable in Victorian times. Women began to wear arrangements of flowers in their hair and pinned to their clothes. Bouquets, small at first but by Edwardian times voluminous, also became necessary accessories.*

The earliest flower shops opened in mid-Victorian times, firstly because there was then wealth to buy flowers. Not old wealth, which had its own estate gardens and garden staff to supply flowers, but new middle-class wealth, which wanted to be fashionable and use flowers for decorating their homes and persons.

Woman with
a Posy *(detail) by*
George Baxter.

The trend for flowers as personal adornment might have begun with Queen Adelaide, wife of William IV, who, it is said, liked to have a bunch of fresh flowers tucked into her waistband or the sash of her dress. Whatever its beginnings, it was in Victorian times that it got well and truly under way – no doubt because nicely made-up fresh flowers look pretty worn or carried but perhaps also because there was then a certain sentimentality attached to flowers. For example, one of the pastimes of ladies was to learn 'the language of flowers'. In this, every flower had a different sentiment attached to it and the way it was given or presented added a further nuance to the 'meaning'. A rose bud given with its thorns and leaves attached meant, 'I fear but I hope' (the thorns implied fear and the leaves hope); with the thorns and leaves off it meant, 'Never to fear nor hope'. With only the thorns removed it implied, 'Fear is to be banished'; however, if thorns were left on and the leaves taken away it warned the receiver that 'There is everything to fear' – it sounds an extremely unpleasant gift. One of the most heartstopping flower gifts a girl could hope for must have been a bouquet of tuberose ('I have seen a lovely girl') and red tulips ('Declaration of love') encircled by fern ('Sincerity').

The fashion for decorating rooms with cut flowers got going around the late 1850s, along with the use of ornamental plants, which nurserymen cultivated in small pots suitable for sitting rooms, windows or tables. Flowers and small pot plants came into their own on the dining table when it became fashionable to dine *à la* Russe. Cassell's *Household Guide* for 1869 describes how this came about:

> The ornamenting of the table has within the last few years received great attention, and has been not only more elegant, but less expensive. Formerly, massive designs in silver, branch candelabra, and silver-mounted épergenes gave due magnificence to the banquet. These, if costly, were heavy. The introduction of the Russian mode of spreading the table with flowers and fruit and either only setting a few dishes on table, or handing them all, which is the true mode *à la* Russe, has brought amongst us graceful ornaments of glass, pyramids of exquisitely chaste crystal – light airy, sparkling and fragrant with blossoms.

Opposite: A reconstruction of Victorian dinner table decoration, following the advice given in a journal dated June 1861 that says that anemones look striking in artificial light.

In wealthy establishments the decoration of the dining table was done by the head gardener with flowers from the walled garden but in lesser households the lady of the house saw it as one of her 'decorative arts'. She could purchase the likes of lilies, lapageria, orchids, jasmine sprays, grasses, graceful ferns and potted crotons or small palms from her local florist. Popular manuals gave advice on decorating – for example: 'Anemones are very lovely for a dinner table. They blaze out in the

Visitors at a fashionable flower show.

brilliant light and really become a most striking spectacle.' A visit to a large flower show could also generally give useful tips, for there was usually a class called 'Table Decoration'. This class included examples of dinner tables set with cutlery and glass-ware and decorated with flowers, grasses and ferns. The best effort won a prize.

At plant nurseries, propagations from newly imported plants, improvements in glasshouse structure and glasshouse heating systems, and better methods of trans-port all helped the production of plants and flowers and their delivery to markets and florists' shops. Thus, public interest in flowers and plants was well fuelled. Indeed, some patrons of flower shops could get carried away. For example, at an

1871 bankruptcy proceedings, proof of a bill for £353 was submitted (presumably by a florist) for flowers supplied to the unfortunate bankrupt over a period of six months. Included in the bill was a £150 charge for lilies of the valley and fern and, rather shockingly, 10s 6d for an individual Moss rose. Well, I suppose the rose might have been worth it, for according to the language of flowers a Moss rose sent the message 'Voluptuous love'!

It was against the background of all these trends and circumstances that the rise of the flower shop began.

❊

CHAPTER ONE

The first florists

The history of florists can be confusing, for up until about 1870 if someone referred to a 'florist' they didn't mean what we understand the term to mean today: a person who sells and arranges flowers in a flower shop. They might have meant either a flower-growing 'enthusiast'; a nurseryman growing outdoor flowers for market; or a nurseryman who specialized in growing and selling or hiring, exotic or greenhouse plants. However, all three of these in their different ways had a bearing on the history of the flower shop.

Florist 'enthusiasts' devoted special attention to improving plants by cultivation, careful selection and systematic hybridization. Their aim was perfection in shape and colouring. Among the flowers they worked with, the most popular were auriculas, carnations, chrysanthemums, cinerarias, dahlias, fuchsias, gladioli, pelargoniums and tulips.

Some of the first florists in England were Flemish worsted manufacturers who had been driven to Norwich by persecution in their own country. There is a record of a 'Florists' Feast' – a gathering to dine, discuss and exhibit flowers – at Norwich in 1637.

These early florists were working men who tempered daily toil with relaxation and interest in flowers – a tradition that has endured. One of the most famous florists in Victorian times was Benjamin Simonite of Rough Bank Smithy in Sheffield. He worked with a mate in a shed in his garden: the mate beat out on an anvil the shape of table knives from steel bars and Benjamin rounded, flattened and shaped them on a grindstone before delivering them to a cutlerer. In any free time he had Benjamin tended and shielded carnations, auriculas and tulips which he grew in windswept plots around the smithy. Besides part-time florists, there were nurserymen like Charles Turner of the Royal Nurseries, Slough, who was well known for his auriculas and devoted his time to raising and perfecting flowers for sale.

Florists prepared the flowers they exhibited at shows with great care. They removed dust from them with camel-haired brushes, tweaked out unsightly petals with tweezers and carefully arranged the remaining petals with a bodkin so that a flower looked at its very best. Thomas Hogg, writing in 1830, gives an insight into this process:

Opposite: A detail from The Flower Arrangement *by Henry Maynell Rheam. Women working in flower shops have long provided artists with a pleasing subject but the paintings give no indication of the damp, chilly conditions necessary, to this day, for such work.*

Christopher Nunn of Enfield, Middlesex, a noted florist of his day, was eminent for his skill and dexterity in dressing Pinks and Carnations for prize exhibition; some will even tell you that Kit was father of the art. Upon such occasions he has as many applications to dress flowers as he had to dress wigs, for he was a barber and friseur by trade, and with all a good-natured, facetious, prating barber, and could both shave and lay a Carnation with the greatest nicety.

Inevitably, improved flowers stopped being exclusive to florists but were grown by nurserymen as well and thus entered into the currency of flowers for sale.

From early times there were, particularly in London, nurseries which had show houses and supplied gentlemen's gardens with plants, seeds and sundries. Some even took in sick plants from customers and nursed them back to health. Another side of their trade was hiring out pot plants. John Loudon writes, in the 1834 edition of his *Encyclopaedia of Gardening*, of plants being sent out to decorate 'midnight assemblages called routs'. He adds: 'This is the most lucrative part of the grower's business, who generally receives half the value as the plants lent out, as many of them, and generally those of most value, are inured by the heat as never to recover.' Such a nursery was Colley and Hill which, at the beginning of Queen Victoria's reign, had a frontage in King Street in London and its grounds extended up towards the Mall and overlooked the River Thames. As well as exotic plants it stocked auriculas, dahlias, verbenas, chrysanthemums, fuchsias and roses.

Lee and Kennedy of the Vineyard Nursery in Hammersmith specialized in new and rare plants; the first China rose was exhibited at their nursery in the late 1780s. Benjamin S. Williams grew exotic and greenhouse plants (amaryllis being a speciality) at the Victoria and Paradise Nursery in Upper Holloway. On the King's Road, Chelsea, were Bull's, who styled itself as New Plant Merchants, and James Veitch & Son, of the Royal Exotic Nursery. Veitch had a large collection of orchids and supplied bouquets made from its blooms and those of other exotic plants.

Until the second half of the nineteenth century the majority of land close to the cities was worked by market gardeners. But as the newly well-off middle classes became able to afford 'villa' type houses built in the suburbs, cities spread out. Around London, builders offered up to £5,000 per acre and many owner-occupiers sold to them. Tenants found that as the value of the ground rose, so did their rents, and they too left. So it was that the large tracts of land which had been fruit and vegetable market gardens became houses, and growers moved further out and began to rely on the improving methods of transport to get their goods to the city markets.

However, this was not the case with many nurserymen growing plants and flowers, who didn't need a large amount of land on which to grow their produce and could get by with a smallish tract of open ground and, say, half an acre of glasshouses. The suburban villas spread around them and the householders were good customers. They wanted bedding plants for their gardens, pot plants for their rooms and the occasional bunch of cut flowers. Nurserymen who, before starting up their own businesses had been head gardeners on large estates, could also offer customers the skills of bouquet and wreath making which they had learnt while in private service.

An interesting illustration of the increasing trade for flowers is shown by the expansion of the Shoults' nursery business. In the 1861 census for Finchley, George B. Shoults of Ballards Lane is described as a 23-year-old florist employing a man and a boy. In the 1871 census his address is given as Rowsley Villa, Alexandra Grove (which sounds a grander address than Ballards Lane) and he was employing five men, four boys and had an 18-year-old live-in apprentice florist.

Sales from a nursery were usually done at a bench in one of the outbuildings but some nurseries had a shop. For example, as early as the 1850s Cuthberts of Southgate, Edmonton, had a shop in South Street which was looked after by the wife of one of the sons of the family. The shop probably sold seed, plants, a few cut flowers and some fruit, for the nursery had a reputation for forced strawberries.

Many London nurserymen who sold produce from their premises also had a stand in Covent Garden flower market. They would arrive at the market about midnight and by 1.00 a.m. selling would be at its height, with the road almost impassable because of the crush of basket women and costermongers buying cut flowers and flowering pot plants to hawk around the streets that day.

By 1851 there were more than four hundred basket women or 'flower girls' on the London streets. Before they set out on their selling routes the flower girls sat on the steps of St Paul's church at Covent Garden or on the steps of houses surrounding the market and divided the large bunches they'd bought into smaller ones. Here they also made up buttonhole bouquets.

An early engraving of London's Covent Garden showing the new central arcade of flower shops.

At about that time, Charles Kenny, an American writer, went to the flower market at Covent Garden and wrote of what he saw:

> Towards the afternoon the bouquet girl is in the height of her ministry. Her delicate fingers are now engaged in trickling out the loveliness of nature for even her loveliest daughters must be drilled and trained ere they can make their debut in the world of artifice they are called upon to adorn. Their slender stems need a wiry support to prop the head that else would droop in the oppressive atmosphere of the ballroom or the theatre.

It is not clear whether he is writing about street flower sellers; probably he is not, for it is unlikely that he would have arrived before dawn, by which time they would have long since departed with their bunches of flowers. It is more likely, especially as he described a 'bouquet girl', that he was observing one of the shops which formed a grand row down the centre of the flower market. If this is so, it could be one of the earliest descriptions of a florist – in the sense of some-one selling flowers – at work in a shop.

There is speculation as to how it was that women came to work with flowers. One theory is that the first women florists were ladies' maids who for some reason or another had left private service but retained their skills at making up bouquets and sprays of flowers for ladies to wear. Attempting to find their own way in the world, they bought flowers, fash-ioned them into made-up pieces at their homes or lodgings and sold them in the streets. They might also have had regular customers who wanted flowers as personal adornment but could not afford to employ a full-time ladies' maid.

An engraving showing a woman at work among cut flowers and plants.

The theory goes on to see the ex-ladies' maid buying her flowers from one nurseryman, and he, sensing the potential of her bringing him regular orders, starts to employ her full-time. In 1865, Henry Mayhew, who wrote *Shops and Companies of London*, refers to a lady called Mary Johnson as having a flower shop in Central Avenue, Covent Garden; whether this is how she began is a matter for conjecture.

The Gardener's Record of 26 February 1870 gives the following fulsome description of Covent Garden flower shops:

> What a display of flowers is here! And what an amount of taste is displayed by those flower-girls in the first-class flower shops, in the making of those ball, court, and wedding bouquets! No gardener need be ashamed to pick up a wrinkle or two here in the art of bouquet-making, for I believe nowhere in the world are bouquets put up with better taste than here.

WEARER AND MAKER.

WEALTHY, and young, and fair,
With the sun's own gold in her shining hair,
With the coral's rose-dye on cheeks and lips,
And eyes whose blue radiance finds eclipse
In lashes of ebon darkness ; around,
Rich Parian mirrors that touch the ground
Reflect her every charm—
From her graceful head to her tiny feet,
Dimpled shoulder and rounded arm,
Perfectly splendid and complete.
On the lace-hung table before her, lie
Flowers and perfumes, and jewellery,
In dainty cases of opal and gold,
Rare as the delicate treasures they hold.
Diamonds gleam 'midst her tresses, bright
As stars in the evening's golden light ;
Robed in white satin that, fold upon fold,
Floats round her like moonbeams—as pure and cold ;
Ready with murmur, with glance, and with smile,
The heart to wreck and the soul to beguile.
Each night for feasting, each morning for play—
The rich robes hide bravely the feet of clay !

Certainly these flower-girls beat our French neighbours hollow in this respect, all that may be said to the contrary notwithstanding. One or two girls are employed putting the flowers on wires, another one, who appears to be forewoman, makes up the bouquets with great quickness, taste, and effect. Much of the effect is due to the employment only of a few decided and pleasing colours. As a rule, they are most effective where no attempt has been made to introduce fern fronds or any other such green material in the centre of the bouquets; fern fronds, leaves of the cut-leaved geranium, &c., being generally used for an edging. Many ladies now object to the Maiden Hair fronds in ball bouquets, as they drop so soon . . .

There are a good many orchid flowers in some of the shops, the fine old *Dendrobium nobile* being most plentiful. Buttonhole bouquets seem to be in great demand, and are very well done. The principal flowers used in their formation just now are red and white clove carnations, pieces of white hyacinths, rose buds, cyclamens, scarlet geraniums, Lily of the Valley, violets, orchid flowers, and Maiden Hair fern. There were a fine lot of cyclamens in seven inch pots for sale, splendid plants with bulbs as large as one's fist, with fine foliage, and hundreds of flowers on each plant. Cinerarias are in abundance, and are pretty well done, the plants being dwarf and healthy with fine heads of bloom.

Tulips and hyacinths also are in abundance. I did not notice a bit of white forced lilac in any of the flower shops.

A few other flower shops started in the heart of London. It is believed that they catered for those inhabitants of well-to-do areas who did not want to travel out to suburban florists' nurseries and also felt that Covent Garden was an inconvenient distance away.

It is difficult to find out who these early London florists were but a book published in 1951 provides an interesting lead. The book, *Commercial Glasshouse Crops*, is, as its title suggests, mainly about the growing of commercial glasshouse crops but at one point its author Dr W. F. Bewley writes about where people could have bought glasshouse plants in central London. He mentions nurseries such as Veitch and Bull's but says there were few other places. He then goes on to state:

Florists' shops were also rare, but about 1857 such firms as Green, Strudwick and Wills came into prominence. Sometime between 1840 and 1850 there lived one, Charles Wood, a bookbinder by trade. Bookbinders' shops were never attractive at the best of times, and Wood sought to

Opposite: Ladies' maids had to have the skill to make and attach floral accessories.

brighten his by bringing flowers from his garden and displaying them in his window. So many people asked to purchase them that Wood saw the possibilities of a florist's shop and gradually developed into a grower and seller of flowers.

Unfortunately Dr Bewley gave no references for this information. Wills must refer to John Wills, a famous floral decorator of Onslow Crescent; Green, Strudwick and Wood were certainly unknown to me at the time I read Dr Bewley's book.

I wrote to the Institute of Bookbinding and Allied Trades asking if they had any record of a Charles Wood practising bookbinding in London between the 1840s and 1850s, and Tony Clark kindly came up with the following: 'Charles Wood was a trade binder operating from 21 High Street, Marylebone, from 1840 to 1852 (the dates are as close as I can get). He did not produce anything that would be classed as collectable.' A trade binder is apparently one who works mainly for local printers and binding houses and doesn't do rebinds or restoration work, so it is quite likely, that, as Dr Bewley suggests, Wood would not have had a very attractive window – that is, no lovely old bound volumes to display.

On the day Mr Clark's letter arrived, I was looking through some garden journals of the 1870s. In *The Gardener's Chronicle and Agricultural Gazette* for 2 July 1870 there was an account of a rose show at the Crystal Palace, which said:

> In addition to the show of Roses an additional treat was provided in the form of a display of table decoration showing three different styles of ornament in a *diner à la Russe,* arranged in the new opera room, which was fitted up in the fashion of a banquet ball for the purpose. Mrs Dickson, Covent Garden, and Mrs Green, Crawford Street, Bryanston Square, both contributed very tasteful arrangements.

Mrs Green? Then, the *Journal of Horticulture and Cottage Gardener* for 8 May 1877 produced every ace in the pack. On 2 May the Royal Horticultural Society staged a big summer show. It was thought to be the most remarkable exhibition that had ever been seen in England (and probably anywhere else). Queen Victoria and a large royal party attended and everyone who was anyone in the horticultural world put in exhibits in an attempt to win prizes. Under the section headed 'Table Decorations and Bouquets' was a string of London individuals and companies, among whom were Messrs. Green & Co., Victoria Street, SW; Mr G. Strudwick, 20 Bayswater Terrace; and Chas. Wood & Sons, 21 High Street, Manchester Square. All won major awards.

There was also mention of a Mr S. Moyses of 22 Stockbridge Terrace, Belgravia; and a Miss Moyses of the same address is listed as winning an award for bouquet making in a show held one month later. These two must be the founder members of Moyses Stevens, the florists currently in Sloane Street, who give the date the firm became established as 1876.

There was indeed a firm called Robert Green & Co. at Bryanston Square, so the bouquet maker Mrs Green was probably Robert Green's wife. Subsequent research has also brought to light that Green's began trading in approximately 1860 and continued to be amongst the élite of florists for many years, becoming well known for its floral decorations of interiors and exteriors. During the preparations for the 1937 coronation the firm festooned the Ministry of Health's tall building at Whitehall with rounded garlands made of magnolia leaves. A quarter of a million leaves were prepared for the garlands and steeplejacks had to be hired to hang the completed decorations.

Green's company last traded under the name of Robert Green, Gerard Ltd, in Maida Vale. Locals recall the florist's shop, which had a glasshouse at the rear. Both shop and glasshouse have now gone and houses are being built on the site. The name has also finally gone, for the company was bought by Strouds, Floral Decorators of Rochester Square.

G. Strudwick of 20 Bayswater Terrace, mentioned by Dr Bewley as a well-known Victorian florist, remains a mystery, for I have not come across his name apart from that mention of it in 1877 and Bayswater Terrace is no longer a road in London street directories.

What of Charles Wood? As there is no High Street in Manchester Square and the nearest High Street is Marylebone's, just above Manchester Square, the 1877 reference is more than likely to be the bookbinder mentioned by Dr Bewley, now trading as a florist with his sons. In the 1885 Marylebone Trades Directory, Charles Wood & Sons are listed as still trading as florists from 21 High Street, Marylebone, but by 1900 the firm's address is given as 22 and 23 High Street, Marylebone. Whether it still had No. 21 but was using it for residential purposes alone is not known. Today, Nos. 21 and 23 share a large wooden doorway and there is no sign of a shop at all. Above the doorway, there are what appear to be flats; the brick exterior of the building looks newer than the old parts of Marylebone High Street. It needs a vivid imagination to see instead of the wooden doorway a dim bookbinder's window, brightened by a vase of flowers – one of the first ever flower shops.

John Wills, the fourth florist mentioned by Dr Bewley, was perhaps the most well-known London florist of the Victorian age. He was born in 1832 at Chard in Somerset. He came to London and worked for various private gardens and also for nurseries. In 1874 he was described as 'one of our most extensive floral decorators' and few London functions or major shows were without his stunning creations. These often involved huge blocks of ice in the form of obelisks or rockeries with fountains and striking displays of palms and other foliage plants. On one commission to decorate the Mansion House he used two tons of ivy to drape mirrors and pictures and 2,000 blooms of Marechal Neil rose, plus large quantities of sweet-scented flowers and palms, pandanuses, marantas, aralias and orchids. Wills often made bouquets for Queen Victoria and the royal princesses and in 1877 when the Prince of Wales moved into Marlborough House he was appointed to keep that establishment supplied with floral decoration.

An interesting example of Wills's ability to 'think big' was a design he drew up in 1877 for an immense glass structure to cover the Albert Memorial.

However, Wills's artistic ability outran his finances. By 1882 a business he was involved in called the General Horticultural Company (John Wills) Ltd, which traded on the site where Liberty's presently has its shop in Regent Street, became insolvent. So he accepted money from and joined in partnership with a man called Samuel Moor Segar.

James Segar (or Jim, as he is generally known), grandson of Samuel Segar, explains how his grandfather came to start the partnership:

> Grandfather was a working man, probably from a farming family out of London, who had worked at William Bull's nursery in King's Road. His sister ran a laundry and made money from it. John Wills was no businessman. He got into money difficulties. In 1882 Grandfather borrowed £1,000 from his sister and negotiated a partnership with Wills. On settlement day he had 1,000 golden sovereigns on the table, which he handed over to Wills.

Samuel Moor Segar, who became John Wills's partner in 1882.

The new firm of Wills & Segar was sited at the Royal Exotic Nursery and Floral Establishment, in Onslow Crescent, London, a short distance from South Kensington tube station. Samuel lived at 16 Onslow Crescent, the house immediately to the left of the cut flower department. The entrance to the large glasshouses at the Royal Exotic had 1882 engraved on its portal, so they may have been built at this time or it may be that improvements were made then, for Wills had owned the nursery for some years prior to the partnership.

Fronting the Royal Exotic Nursery and Floral Establishment were the imposing, glass-covered 'Winter Gardens', where visitors could stroll. In addition to these, the nursery, of glass-palace proportions, had a palm show house in which

BIRD'S-EYE • VIEW • OF • OUR • ROYAL • EXOTIC • NURSERY,

A bird's-eye view of the Royal Exotic Nursery premises – an illustration from one of Wills and Segars' old catalogues.

customers could consider palms and then buy them in sizes varying from a few inches to thirty feet in height. There were also fern houses, displays of foliage plants, cut-flower rooms and a glasshouse 140-feet long by 40-feet wide which had been at one time set aside especially to accommodate and take care of plants whose owners were temporarily absent from town.

It was a successful union. Below the name on the entrance of the firm's premises a large royal coat of arms denoted that the firm held a royal warrant. It was awarded this on 28 February 1885 (a company has to supply the royal household for three years before being awarded a warrant) and went on to hold eight in total, the last dated 1950.

Patrick Segar, Jim's son, showed me one of the firm's catalogues from the 1890s. It gives an idea of the large scope of services offered. It advertises wreaths,

Patrick Segar, Samuel Moor Segar's great-grandson.

Literature sent out by the London firm of Wills and Segar showing their proud possession of the royal warrant. The first, awarded in 1875, was followed by another eight during their long history.

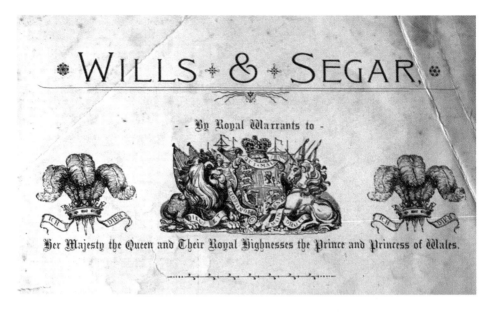

bouquets, and floral decoration for cakes, churches and mansions; and outlines collections of potted plants. For example, there were palms suitable for decorating conservatories, winter gardens, drawing rooms, lawns, terraces, entrance halls and, of course, dinner tables. Ornamental foliaged plants such as dracaenas, caladiums and crotons were 'specially grown in suitable sizes for dinner table decoration'.

Decorating on a much larger scale was also catered for and one page of the catalogue lists the firm's recent assignments. These included:

> The opening of Sheffield Public Park by HRH The PRINCE OF WALES, when the RAILWAY STATION and ROYAL HOTEL were most elaborately decorated. TWENTY-FIVE RAILWAY TRUCK LOADS OF PLANTS, CUT-FLOWERS, etc being used … the GREAT BALL at the MANSION HOUSE on the occasion of the MARRIAGE of HRH The DUKE OF EDINBURGH … and the DECORATIONS at CHARING CROSS RAILWAY STATION on the return of the late LORD BEACONSFIELD from Berlin, when the whole of the enormous platform was converted into a Palm Grove.

The firm also built rockeries and waterfalls, either temporary (for balls etc.) or permanent, and some small enough to fit into window ferneries – and as most window ferneries were usually no more than a smallish glass case fitted to the outside of a window, these *must* have been small.

❊

London was probably the first city to have 'exclusive' florists' shops – that is, shops whose proprietors bought most, if not all, of the flowers they sold from the markets and did not grow them themselves – but, of course, other parts of Britain also had their early flower sellers, of which there are a number of notable examples.

In Manchester in the 1850s you could buy single blooms or bouquets of flowers at Mr Yates's premises in St Ann's Square. Mr Yates was also a confectioner and a fruiterer. The fruit and flowers came from his nurseries at Sale, half a dozen miles from Manchester. Even in winter his forcing houses provided cut flowers of lilac, deutzias, rhododendrons and lilies of the valley. A horticulturist visiting the nursery in 1858 was particularly struck by a house of camellias being grown for cut flowers. They were mostly double whites, and a thousand blooms were ready for cutting on the day of his visit. Mr Yates had in his nursery the largest stock of the winter-flowering orchid *Coelogyne cristata* in Britain. However, his particular love was acacias, of which again he had the largest collection in the country. Two of these trees were so big that they had to have glasshouses all to themselves. Mr Yates appears to have been an entertaining individual, for when he showed the larger of these two trees to the visitor he said: 'That stem will soon yield boards broad enough to make my coffin, and I intend it for that purpose; or else

Through to Edwardian times and beyond, forced lily of the valley was a sought after crop.

my Deodar [which was on his lawn] shall have the privilege of containing my mortal remains.'

Anyone wanting flowers in Dublin in the 1860s could have patronized Mr Kirkby, fruiterer and florist. He had premises in Sackville Street, Nassau Street and Killester. In Cork there were a number of local nurseries, one of which, Saunders & Sons of Friars Walk, had been trading since 1823. During the latter half of the century, Saunders was offering (in addition to fruit trees and rose bushes), cut flowers, bridal and ball bouquets, sprays (i.e., corsages), wreaths, crosses and 'chaste designs for mortuary flowers'. Customers from further afield could be sent flowers by rail or parcel post.

In Cardiff, what were to become two flower-selling dynasties started up business in the city in the same year – 1850. The shops of the Case and Treseder families have endured almost to the present day. (I write 'almost' for Jonathan Case, the fourth-generation florist in that family, has, rather poignantly and perhaps fittingly, sold his shop to Mrs Cheryl Hopkins, the fourth-generation florist of the Treseder family.)

*Above: Frederick Case.
Below: William Treseder.*

A century and a half ago, Fred Case, a Somerset farmer's son, opened his fruit and flower shop in the High Street, and William Treseder, son of a Cornish nurseryman, began his nursery on land his father had purchased from the Marquis of Bute. In the early years the Treseder nursery concentrated on trees more than flowers, so Mr Case was at that time a surer provider of flowers. He had nurseries at Rumney and in the hothouses there he grew exotic flowers and choice fruits such as grapes, peaches and nectarines. He quickly became established as a first-class florist but it was his fruit which brought him local notoriety. He had two banana trees in full fruit outside his shop and so many people came to see them that the police had to regulate the crowds and he was asked to pay a nominal fine. Some time later there was a further stir outside the shop, this time concerning his tomatoes. He had the distinction of being the first tomato grower in South Wales. Apparently, some miners from the Welsh valleys saw the tomatoes for sale in the window and, thinking they were plums, went in and bought some. When they got outside they bit into them and were so disgusted by the taste that they pelted them against the window.

Such behaviour would have shocked the residents of the genteel spa town of Cheltenham. The resort had good nurseryland on its outskirts and ready trade for fruit and flowers at the town's many florists and fruiterers – it was later to pride itself on being known as 'the Garden Town'.

A 1900 *Town Guide* tells readers that Miss Holder, florist of 10 Pittville Street had 'metaphorically' gathered flowers for the habitués of Pittville Spa for nearly half a century and 'thereby heightened the effects of the brilliant scenes for which the "Pittville" is renowned'; also that her 'artistic handling of each individual flower' rendered her bouquets exceedingly attractive. Mr Phillips, florist and fruiterer at 422 High Street, had a 'floral wealth' of wreaths, crosses, cut flowers, nosegays and bouquets. All were 'of the most beautiful flowers arranged in various effective designs, with the colours harmonized in a highly artistic manner.' His shop also displayed specimens of wedding bouquets, which were made up on the premises: 'The assistants are ever busy with deft fingers and trained taste in the selection and composition of these and similar choice productions for balls, private parties, banquets, etc.'

In addition to selling flowers from their shops, both Miss Holder and Mr Phillips hired out pots of plants for the many society functions that took place in the town during 'the season'. However, their contribution to these functions was small beer compared with the efforts of James Cypher of the Exotic Nurseries in Queen's Road. From 1848 Mr Cypher had been head gardener (in Cheltenham) to a Miss Savage but on her death in the early 1860s he began his own business. Eventually he had seventy large glasshouses, between sixty and seventy staff, and was renowned for his floral decorations. At Assembly Room balls it was Cypher's

> Florists' shops are a sign of the general prosperity of the people because their trade may be regarded more in the light of a luxury of art and taste than as an actual necessity.
>
> *Commercial Gardening*, John Weathers, 1913

Left: An early photograph of a florists' shop. Note the palms and pot plants favoured for room and table decoration.

Overleaf: At the turn of the century the orchid was very popular and J. Cypher and Sons, nurserymen and florists of Cheltenham, excelled in their cultivation and even supplied them to overseas buyers.

Royal Horticultural Society Exhibition at Birmingham, June 25th to 29th

TABLE DECORATIONS

First prize awarded to Mr Cypher, Queen's Road Nursery, Cheltenham, for an exceedingly attractive arrangement. It consists of three March stands, the centre one surrounded by a border of glass, containing flowers and Maidenhair Fern. The bottom circle of the stand is composed of Ixoras and *Eucharis amazonica*, the upper one of Heaths and small Roses, with a plentiful supply of grasses. The dishes of fruit are handsome. At the head and foot are a Pine Apple and Melon, surrounded with a trough containing flowers. The glass is good and appropriate.

Journal of Horticulture and Cottage Gardener, 27 June 1872

ivy that trailed gracefully down pillars and disappeared discreetly behind a palm on a pedestal, and his large flower boxes and rows of garden vases that ornamented the balconies and galleries. The console tables in the crush room laden with flowers and palms were his work too, not to mention the grottoes that were made in large windows and fitted with statuary and a profusion of exotic plants.

Mr Cypher's talents spread beyond Cheltenham and he won prizes for exhibits and table decoration at major flower shows all over the country. His great-great-nephew, Ron Cypher, remembers hearing talk in the family of how big palms in pots and other plants and floral decorations were loaded into a large caravan and drawn by two horses to shows as far afield as Manchester. 'There was a time,' Ron says proudly, 'when the firm was asked not to compete as they always won. But they still exhibited because people said, "Where are Cypher's?" if they weren't there.'

With such a wealth of glasshouses it was inevitable that in addition to decorating, Cypher's developed a big florist's business. Ron says that the shop was on the road frontage with the glasshouses around and behind it. The firm offered bouquets for weddings, balls, operas and presentations; also sprays, garlands and wreaths for wearing; and chaplets, crosses, anchors, crowns, hearts, harps and stars for funerals. Its specialities were wedding and presentation baskets of choice flowers and gentlemen's coat flowers.

In Maidstone, Kent, in 1867, Wallace Richard Harrison bought a seed and nursery business from a Mr W. M. Hammerton. At that time the premises in the High Street were known as the Kent County Seed Stores. For many years Harrison's sold farm and garden seeds and, no doubt having its own nursery, flowers too, in various forms. By 1900 the flower trade was such that it built seven large greenhouses in the centre of town and was able to offer customers bouquets, sprays, buttonholes, wreaths, crosses etc., 'at a few minutes' notice'.

Luton, Bedfordshire, was known years ago for its hat makers, and its neighbour Dunstable for plant nurseries. The forefathers of retired florist Terry Headey contributed to both trades. His great-grandfather used to travel around and buy straw plaits for the hat makers and his grandfather, Alfred George Headey, began a nursery in Dunstable in 1895, styling himself as a 'Florist and Market Grower'.

There was no shop as such, but locals would come to Alfred's potting shed to order wreaths, bunches of chrysanthemums or wedding bouquets, which Alfred, who had trained as a gardener, made up himself. Bedding plants were boxed and collected by the railway horse and flat cart to be taken to the station and from there sent by rail to wholesalers in Birmingham and London. The nursery's own horse and van made local deliveries of flowers and took the nursery carter and salesman to the markets in Aylesbury, Watford and Luton. Aylesbury was fifteen miles away, so the preparation for getting there began the day before. Flowers were cut in the morning, then loaded in the afternoon. The men would set off in the loaded van then stop halfway and overnight at a pub. The next morning they would be at the market at 7.00 a.m. to set up the stall.

It is hard to find a 'local' in Oxford, for the place teems with tourists. However, if you do manage to locate one and you ask if they know of an old florist's business in the city, they'll probably say, 'Joe Austin's'. The firm continues a tradition of flower selling begun by Joe's father, William. In Austin's flower shop on the Cowley Road there is a photograph of a horse-drawn wagon with William in the driving seat. With him is Joe's mother and Joe, as a little boy, standing by the horse's head. On the wagon bed behind them are large baskets filled with flowers. William's granddaughter – Joe's daughter – Janet Carter brings the photo to life:

Austin's of Oxford was founded by William who can be seen driving the cart in this photograph.

Grandfather William had eleven children, seven of whom were girls: Tilley, Biddie, Kate, Lettie, Nelly, Nora and Lily. Each of the girls as they grew old enough, and I think when one got married a younger one would take her place, used to stand on a main street and sell flowers from a basket. There was one in Broad Street, one in the Cornmarket, and another in Cowley Road. In the photo Grandfather is delivering the baskets to their various pitches because they'd be too heavy for the girls to carry.

Grandfather had come from London to live in Oxford and he had a flower shop in the old covered market in the city centre. The market shops in those days didn't have glazing but were open like the present-day fruit shops in the market. The flowers were banked up at the front of the shop. Underneath them was a big tank of water which was filled up every day by the market authorities. Some of the water was taken out for the flowers and the rest used for pot washing. You dipped the pots in and your hands got frozen when you were scrubbing. The market was very cold in winter. The hours used to be long too. Even later when my mother was at the shop they'd stay open till ten o'clock at night and definitely on a Saturday they stayed until they'd sold everything. The market was busy at night with people trying to get a bargain. A lot went purposely late to get meat, fish and fruit not sold and which they knew the shopkeeper would sell off cheaply to get rid of it.

Grandfather lived at New Marsden, which is about three miles from the market. He kept horses in a yard there. When they wanted a fresh horse he went to Stow Horse Fair and, as a boy, my father Joe rode the new horse home. There was a cellar to the house and that's where he kept flowers. He didn't grow any but used to go to Covent Garden on the train and when he brought them back they'd be picked up by the horse and cart. Because he went to market he was a kind of wholesaler and my mum used to go round to other florists in Oxford and take their orders.

Janet became the third generation of the Austins to practice floristry. Indeed, I was to discover that long-standing family businesses seemed to be something of a trait in the trade.

❀

CHAPTER TWO

Inside the earliest flower shops

The following description was written about 125 years ago by an Englishman when he had visited a flower shop on an October evening in Paris. However, it could have passed pretty well for most well-run flower shops in Victorian and Edwardian Britain:

The little shop itself was quite a picture; it was a bower of Palms, Ferns and plants in bloom. Pots of white Lilac, Roses, Pinks and Carnations shed a delightful perfume. Two or three girls were occupied in making bouquets and garlands while the presiding deity, a stout, middle-aged woman with a good-natured face, waited on customers, at the same time superintending the workers.

In those days there would have been more pot plants than cut flowers on display, especially when frosts severed the supply of outside-grown cut flowers. At that time not all growers forced flowers, having decided that it did not pay in winter because 'establishments' were not in town for that season and, to quote from a journal of the day, 'The only trade for flowers was theatre-going people … and … young swans or cygnets of the city.' Fog, too, heavy with soot, could lay a deadly hand on outside flowers and block the light from those in glasshouses. The early months of 1880 were particularly bad for both. One London nurseryman, Henry Benjamin May, had a large stock of the Chinese primrose, *Primula sinensis*, a greenhouse plant about nine inches high with smallish white or pale lilac flowers. To fill the gap he decided to offer these as a cut flower. So keen was the demand that customers queued up each morning at his lodgings and, happily for him, 'murmured not at the unusual prices that prevailed'.

A retired florist writing in the early 1950s paints a further picture of the lack of flowers in winter:

> Even after the end of Victoria's reign, florist's shops in January had little in view beyond Geranium bloom, scarlet and white … there were Roman Hyacinths, Lily-of-the-Valley, some Narcissi, Callas, with the rare appearance of a few Orchids. Violets we had, and I seem to remember single Anemones … Memory supplies a picture of a little colour among a wealth of greenery during January. Ferns were an important part of the florist's stock during the winter months.

At times of the year when cut flowers were plentiful, early flower sellers made up their bouquets with string, for florists' wires did not come into general use until the 1840s. The string method, later known to florists as the 'old or natural style', had the disadvantage that choice flowers were packed between other flowers and crushed, and as a result the bouquet could look a confused mass. A contemporary description of French bouquet making gives an insight into how these early bouquets were constructed. It seems that fancy cord or fine whip cord was attached to the first flower, then a couple more flowers added and the string passed around them a few times. The packed flowers were held by the thumb until another flower was pressed against them and the string then passed round it, and thus the bouquet was built up. Sometimes damp moss was bound on too, to keep the flowers fresh. Some florists had an iron prong attached to a 'dress board' and if they pushed the bouquet on to the prong it left both hands free to arrange and separate the flowers and they could turn the bouquet to look at it from all sides during the making.

It seems, too, that French florists rendered flowers with broken stems, or no stems at all, usable by fixing false stems on to them. They used Spanish yellow rushes, which they bought by the pound. A girl took a rush, doubled it over, put the stemless flower at the point of doubling, connected the flower to the rush with a thread and covered it with a green tuft of moss. The flower on its artificial stem could be laced together in the bouquet like a naturally stemmed one. No doubt other early bouquetists had similar tricks.

It would appear that the early florist's workbench had little more than moss, willow frames, rushes and twine. However, by the 1870s florists were employing at least half a dozen kinds of wire to help them with their work. For example, stout wire had taken the place of a rush or willow wand as an artificial stem and very thin wire, either plain or silverplated and sold on wooden reels, was used to bind flowers on to their artificial wire stems. Fine steel wire in seven-inch lengths was used for piercing camellias or other flowers with short stalks. Also wires of different thickness, depending on the size of the flower, were used to push up inside the stems to make them stronger and more malleable.

It is believed that these florists' wires first came to Britain with French ladies' maids. The maids had used them at home for making up their mistresses' bouquets and personal floral decorations and brought them with their other belongings as a matter of course when they came to work in British households. Gardeners learnt the skill of using the wires from the ladies' maids and later they came into use in florists' shops.

Wires enabled florists to turn any small floret or short-stemmed flower into bouquet or posy material. Indeed during times when fresh flowers were scarce this type of material was all they had to work with. This is illustrated by a reminiscence from nurseryman Henry Benjamin May. In his autobiography, *Seventy Years in Horticulture*, looking back to 1876 he writes:

My life-long friend Thomas Rochford when first in business at Tottenham, marketed pips of a small white Pompom Chrysanthemum in punnets, and the contents of a small house realised some twenty pounds. My friend, W.H. Page (long may he flourish), then a junior selling for his father, had flowerets of double Primulas tied in small bunches, as was then the method. With such material, it will be realised wiring was inevitable.

Geranium heads, as they were available all year round, were much used and wired. Unfortunately the petals dropped when knocked, so florists employed gum or 'floral cement' to hold them fast. An interesting example of how geranium blooms tended to shatter is shown in a contemporary account of a talk given by novelist Charles Dickens. It mentions how he held his audience spellbound with his dark, animated looks and scarlet geranium buttonhole, and how, during his spirited readings from his works, the customary buttonhole (as usual) lost more and more of its petals. Obviously no florist's geranium that! One can imagine him at home just before going out plucking off a geranium head and tucking it into his buttonhole.

Concealing the wire stems in bouquets was necessary and florists kept supplies of paper collars for the purpose. Once one was slipped on and pushed up beneath the heads there was no telling that they were not on natural stems. Cheap kinds of collars had glazed or perforated edges and were made in sizes from six to twelve inches in diameter. A funnel-shaped collar was invented as an improvement. It had a glazed card fitted across the aperture to preserve the shape. Like the ordinary collar it was made of perforated paper but there was a choice of finishes – plain, gilt or silvered. It was customary to fringe finer kinds of bouquets with blond (a cheap kind of lace which it was advisable to keep wrapped in blue paper before use to stop it from turning yellow) and to arrange tastefully a better kind of lace over that. The lace collar was finished off with white satin ribbons, bought by florists from a local draper and probably imported from France.

Stems of bouquet flowers were disguised by tinfoil ripped off a roll supported by a wooden roller; or, if a customer could afford it, they were slipped into a bouquet holder. Holders came in various materials. The mid-Victorian florist might have offered ones of glazed plasterboard or wickerwork. At the turn of the century the choice was extended to include embossed silver or gold paper and embossed moire (watered silk). Much more expensive bouquet holders made of precious metal and gems could be bought from jewellers.

During the 1870s buttonhole bouquets and coat flowers began to become very fashionable and florists sold slender glass tubes for them which slotted behind the lapel. Filled with a little water, the tube would help to keep a buttonhole fresh. At first these tubes were plain but by the early 1900s they were being sold in various designs with fancy gilt tops.

In addition to fresh flower bouquets, most florists sold 'makret bunches'. These were ready-made bouquets of dried grasses sold at markets or direct to shops by early florists' suppliers. The grasses included oats, uniola and agrostis, and some were dyed bright or dark green. French moss might be obtained similarly dyed. The method of colouring was relatively simple and a shop could keep up supplies by dyeing its own grasses. The recipe was two parts of boiling water, one ounce of alum and half an ounce of dissolved indigo carmine. The grass or moss was plunged into this mixture, then taken out and shaken and dried in the air in a shady place or, in winter, by fire heat. If light green was wanted, picric acid was added to the mixture; the more acid, the lighter the green.

During the autumn, large amounts of everlasting flowers or 'immortelles' were imported, mainly from the Continent. These could be coloured with a commercial product known as Judson's dye. Florists sold everlastings loose, in sprays for a few shillings, in bouquets, or made up into wreaths and crosses. Helichrysum was used as a dried flower, popularly known in those days as the 'Cape flower' as most species came from South Africa. However, in 1905 the South African crop failed and a paper Cape flower was made in Germany and exported. It quickly became very popular. Incidentally, also in 1905, another preserved flower novelty came to florists' shops: red ruscus, introduced by a sundriesman named William Faust.

From the 1870s, and probably earlier, Germany had exported roses and pelargoniums which had been dried in heat and sand. Also sold and used by florists in those early days were dried and varnished autumn leaves such as maple or oak, and a commodity not vegetative but certainly decorative – peacock feathers.

Shops used an assortment of containers in which to store and display cut flowers, including jam jars, water jugs from toilet sets and the occasional large Japanese vase. Florists' brown and green glaze tubular pottery vases, waisted and with the bases slightly wider than the tops, were available, perhaps from the 1890s. By the 1920s flower sellers could buy solid steel enamelled green buckets and vases. Summer flowers, too large for bouquets or wreaths, such as foxgloves, lilies and gladioli, might have been arranged in an elegant wicker basket and placed in the shop window as a ready-to-give gift.

In Edwardian times there was an enormous trade for gift baskets of flowers. The basket was usually tall and slender. One of the best-known basket makers for florists was Isaac Rich of High Road, Tottenham, in London. He set up business in 1905 and fifty years later, although almost eighty, was still heading the firm.

Most florists offered a number of vases for sale. In mid-Victorian times these included hyacinth vases in glass, terracotta or Etruscan ware and to go with them a metal support which popped into the vase top and held the hyacinth flower spike erect.

Tall, narrow glasses which would take one curious or interesting flower were popular. These were known as specimen vases. Also fashionable were small vases in plain or coloured glass for setting before each guest at the dinner table, filled with a choice flower plus its foliage. Novelty pot covers made in an ivy latticework design would expand to cover earthenware flowerpots which had been brought into the drawing room. When not in use the cover could be rolled up for easy storage. By the 1890s customers could also choose from a range of white china fern- and flowerpots. Some of these were fluted, others made to look like mock wicker and a number shaped like a shell or ship with a Little Boy Blue or Bo-Peep figure stuck firmly to one end.

Early receptacles for grave flowers were generally troughs in the shape of crosses, anchors or wreaths. The first metal grave vase which had a spike and a loose perforated top went on sale in 1905. Also sold for graves were artificial wreaths made of metal and porcelain.

Wrapping paper for purchases from early florists was simple. Mr J. P. Widdup, whose family firm in Bradford has been making packaging for florists (and other businesses) for over a hundred years, says that in the very early years florists used ordinary sheet wrapping paper or tissue, some even used newspaper. A 1926 florists' suppliers catalogue offers tissue paper in white, dark blue, pink and mid-blue, and also white sulphite paper.

If bouquets were being transported they were packed in boxes which had wooden sides and bottoms and stout cardboard lids covered with strong glazed brown paper. Funeral cross boxes were similarly constructed, as were wreath boxes, although – perhaps for greater safety – some wreath boxes had wooden lids instead of cardboard ones. By 1926 wreath boxes were no longer wooden but made of 'collapsible leatherboard'. Wreaths being hand-delivered to their destination might be packed in lined, white card boxes. One wreath case advertised by florists' sundriesmen at the turn of the century resembled a large pocket watch case and is described as a 'wreath case dome' made of 'zinc and English white glass'. For an extra cost you could buy a galvanized wire protector to go with it. This looked like a hanging basket turned upside down and was supported by four spike legs. Presumably the zinc and glass dome (which could be from eight to twenty inches in diameter) was a permanent packaging for a wreath of artificial flowers which would sit upon a grave for as long as fate allowed.

As the introduction of wires in various thicknesses for mounting and binding helped florists to be increasingly artistic with flowers, so wire took its place in other parts of the business. Customers might be treated to a display of wire flowerpot hangers or wire fern baskets suspended on chain handles and in the 'making-up' area there would be stocks of wire wreath foundations. For ease of selection the best way of storing these was on nails on the wall, one design to a nail. It was also less damp than the floor. The designs included harps, anchors, crosses, stars, horseshoes, oval-shaped chaplets, lyres, Maltese crosses, Masonic square and compasses, cushions and circles.

CHAPTER THREE

Learning the craft

Bob Fowler, now ninety-four, has a photograph of his father, Arthur J. Fowler, wearing a straw boater, standing in the doorway of a large, elegant, conservatory-like shop: Scott's florist's of Eastbourne, of which he became the manager in 1898. Arthur Fowler stayed two years at Scott's then moved on to other florists – first to Foster's of Maidstone where he met his wife-to-be, and then to Moore's of Chichester where he married in 1904. He then began to look about for his own shop. Bob takes up the story:

I was eleven months old when Father rented a shop, 62A St Mary's Road, Southampton, in April 1907. It was a two-bedroom house and the shop was built on the front garden and for the next eleven years (until Father bought a house in 1918) we lived in the fairly small living accommodation of the house.

Our workroom was in a sub-basement, three steps down from the flower shop. Most florists seemed to use metal vases painted green in those days but we used glass vases, some quite tall, bought from the Florists' Sundries and Wreath Co., whose traveller was Mr Milner. We had several lengths of glass shelving. There was a wall-mounted phone and you turned a handle to ring the exchange to give the operator the number that you wanted. Orders were entered in a daily ledger and to deal with payment we had a draw till on the counter. We also displayed flowers there. Occasionally we stood a container of flowers in the doorway. The only other items we put outside were holly wreaths and crosses. We always made our own in both silver and golden holly with berries cut out from green holly.

There was a flight of stairs going up from the shop to the house and as we didn't use the stairs we kept *Kentia* palms on them. On the right-hand wall as one entered the shop we had a display of glass domes containing porcelain wreaths for which we had good sales in the 1920s. I believe eventually cemeteries banned them because of broken glass.

In the workroom there were the usual stub wires and binding wire and we each had a penknife. As well as flowers we sold vegetable seeds because of the 1914–18 war.

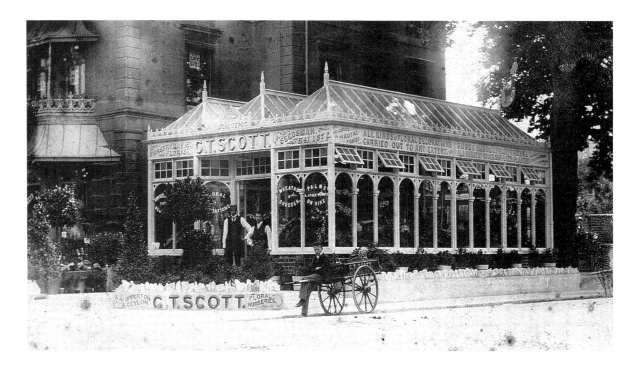

Before that war and into the 1920s there were no wholesale florists in Southampton so my father went twice a week to Covent Garden market. He took the last train at night. The market opened at three o'clock. He'd usually buy flowers and foliage from William Newton and Sons. Large flowers, like chrysanthemums, were sold in big wooden boxes and a three shilling deposit was paid on the box. Roses and carnations had much narrower boxes and there was a shilling deposit on those.

Father would take the boxes of flowers back to Waterloo and catch the 5.40 a.m. train home. This arrived at the Docks station at 8.00 a.m. In those days trams went from the station to St Mary's Road – it was, in fact, the end of the line for them. He put the boxes in the front of the tram behind the driver and when we – for I can remember helping him – got off, we lugged them across the road to the shop.

In 1928 Father purchased some nice premises just across the road and we moved our shop to them. The property had two floors above and a workroom lying quite a long way back. At the rear it had once been a stable and there was a hayrack and stable cobbling, drains and a tap. It was ideal storage for our flowers.

The empty wooden flower boxes from Newton's in Covent Garden had to go back because of the deposit on them. We waited until we got what we considered a full load and then rang Southern Railway who came with a flat-bed lorry. It had a small edging to the bed so when the boxes were put on they could be tipped up a little sideways against this and wouldn't fall off. They used to pile up these boxes and throw a rope over them to help secure them.

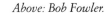

Above: Bob Fowler.

In addition to market flowers, a local nurseryman called Dalrymple used to grow scabious in front of his greenhouses and bring them in, and other local growers supplied violets and asters which were useful in their season in those days. In the 1920s and 1930s we bought forced white lilac direct from P. Eveleens & Sons of Aalsmeer in Holland. It came by boat and train in a cardboard box. We also used to buy white narcissus from France, which arrived in 'pads' made of split bamboo.

Opposite, top: Bob's father, Arthur, standing in the doorway of Scott's of Eastbourne when he was the shop manager.

Opposite, below: The Fowler's shop in Southampton.

In 1923 when Bob was aged seventeen, he left school and went to the Royal Horticultural Society's Wisley Gardens where, in 1925, he gained a diploma in floristry and returned home as a partner in the family business. There had been no need for further training, for, at the time, he was already doing a lot of the practical work and he had, after all, been helping in the workroom from as soon as he was old enough.

Bob Fowler's story not only provides an illuminating description of the work in a flower shop during the early years of the twentieth century but it also illustrates two recurrent themes in the history of the flower shop: that many people went into the business because a parent had been in it before them; and that many florist's businesses flourished over several generations.

John James Cypher (centre) and, to his right, his nephew, Frank Cypher, who took over from his uncle and went on to become managing director.

Cypher's of Cheltenham continued to be run by James Cypher's descendants until it closed in 1960. His great-great-nephew Ron Cypher says that when he was a boy, the nursery was run by his father and his father's brothers and sisters. Ron's aunts worked in the shop making up wreaths, buttonholes and the like, and

the brothers looked after the glasshouses. Ron remembers the amount of personal attention his father gave to customers: 'He'd take ladies down to the greenhouse to select their own individual plants, spend ten minutes or more advising them, because often people made enquiries regarding their gardening problems, and then at the end the plant changed hands for the princely sum of sixpence!' However, Ron's uncle, Frank Cypher (now deceased), recalled a more substantial price tag on a plant. His father, John James Cypher, had built up a massive collection of orchids for which he was renowned and Frank said that one of these, an *Odontoglossum crispum perfectum*, grown from seed at the nursery in the early 1900s, was bought by a customer in Manchester for £1,000. It was carefully packed and sent to him.

Harrison's of Maidstone thrived for almost one and a half centuries. 'In Maidstone, a gift of flowers becomes a mark of social "good taste" when the box bears the tag "From Harrisons"', a 1932 customer's catalogue reminded its customers. This catalogue is among a host of papers relating to the Harrison's long history, belonging to Jonathan Harrison, who has only recently relinquished the family's floristry business begun by his great-grandfather.

A young Joe Austin helping his father with a barrow of flowers ready to sell to their Oxford customers.

When Alfred Headey died in 1930, his son Leslie took over his Dunstable nursery business and when Leslie died in 1950 his son Terry, then aged twenty, took over. He recalls: 'There was a general trend against growing in the 1950s and more money in retail. We opened a florist's shop on the site of the potting shed and in fact at one time had two other florist's shops in town. In the first year the shop took ninety pounds a week, which wasn't very good considering how much it cost to run it!' However, economics aside, the shop was to provide a personal benefit for Terry. A girl called Prue came to work in it on Saturdays. She left but returned, fully trained, several years later to work full-time, and she and Terry married. Eventually the nursery land was sold for development but the shop continued. When Terry and Prue retired, their son, Charles, and his wife took over and today, the potting-shed-site shop is a bright oasis amidst houses and roads.

Joe Austin also followed in his father's footsteps. His daughter Janet Carter explains: 'When Dad married he stopped working with his father and spent a short while working with other florists before getting his own shop in St Aldate's.' Joe's business was to move several times over the years. Eventually Janet and her husband Peter Carter took over from him and now their son Robyn has taken over from them. Robyn still supplies flowers to places such as the colleges which were originally his great-grandfather's customers.

Wills & Segar continued in business until the 1970s and provided a place of training for Samuel Segar's grandson, Jim. Samuel Segar had three sons – Sam, born in 1887, Jack and Frank. Jack was killed in the very last days of the First World War but Frank and Sam kept the business going. Jim is Sam's son, born in 1920, and he remembers playing among large potted plants in the Royal Exotic

Above: Jim Segar, grand-son of Samuel.

Right: The shop at 77 Old Brompton Road.

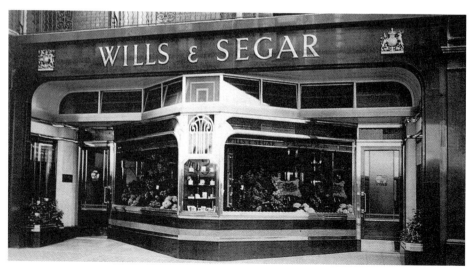

Nursery and Floral Establishment's Winter Gardens. Jim recalls that in his father's time, as well as decorating for court occasions such as investitures, the firm also employed twenty girls and fifteen men who bedded out and tended private gardens.

The Royal Exotic Nursery was demolished in 1933. In retrospect Jim, who was then thirteen, believes this was a good thing, for all the glass would have been a liability during the Second World War. He says:

That year we took 77 Old Brompton Road on a thirty-year lease. It cost ten thousand pounds to set up – which was a large amount of money in those days. Curved windows were put in. My father didn't really want them because he thought they weren't a good idea. It was supposed to be that you could almost seem to reach in to the flowers but anyone looking in was six feet back!

A small refrigerated room was also put in. It was necessary, for if you had a busy weekend you could do flowers ahead and put them in the cool.

Father's motto with my sister and myself was: 'Take them young and treat them rough.' When I was about sixteen I went to Tim Hillings Nursery at Chobham. It specialized in outdoor shrubs. I got five shillings a week and lodged as a jobbing gardener. It helped me mix with people – there were miners there from Wales because the prospects in horticulture were better then than in mining and I learnt how to stand up for myself. After that I went to Luff's of Wimbledon who were landscape people, learnt how to bricklay etc., then came the war.

My cousin Cyril, Jack's boy, joined me in running the business. He had been trained in Paris by Baumann; learning about flowers and the French language at the same time. I did the buying and Cyril, with his florist's training, ran the shop.

Uncle Frank had been the market man in my father's day. I went with him, then continued on my own. At the height of business I'd go to bed twice a day. I went to the market at 3.00 a.m. then I'd go back to the shop to sort out the material I'd bought. At 1.00 p.m. I went home, put pyjamas on and went to bed. At 4.00 p.m. I'd go back to

The preliminary stage of training is perhaps least tempting, for it involves long, tiring hours spent in a hot, unrestful florist's shop. It will be found best to serve an apprenticeship in this way for some months. Possibly the people met there are not very obliging or polished; often work has to be done under extreme pressure, as many orders have to be ready at the same moment, and the freshness of flowers has to be greatly considered. Bouquets, dinner-tables, all have to be postponed until the last safe moment. Consequently there remains but little time for enjoyment of completed work, and there is very scant appreciation ... The premium for acquiring experience is a heavy one. It varies according to the position and reputation of the florist's shop, but it is never less than fifteen pounds, and it often reaches fifty pounds. During the first year it is not usual to obtain a salary ... Only those who have tried it know what tiring work flower arrangement is, and only strong, able-bodied girls should contemplate such a profession.

Gardening for Women Hon. Frances Wolseley, 1907

the shop and work out what flowers were needed for the next day's business so that I could do a buying order. It was a very disturbing regime.

When the lease ran out on 77 Old Brompton Road in 1974 the firm moved to 94 Old Brompton Road. That shop closed when Jim was seventy. However, Jim's son Patrick Segar carries on the family tradition of floristry as a profession and is now the fourth generation of the family to be in floristry. He has a business at London's Canary Wharf, called Felton, Wills & Segar, and his partner, Richard Felton, also comes from several generations of florists.

Right up until the time that Wills & Segar closed, Jim had stuck to a custom begun in Covent Garden market in John Wills's time: 'Because of John Wills's financial difficulties, the market wholesalers wouldn't do business with him on credit – they'd only take cash. Wills & Segar continued to pay cash up until my retirement!'

Wills & Segar was among a number of well-known florists who took apprentices, whose parents paid a weekly sum for their son or daughter to get practical experience and learn from professionals. Robin Wayne of Swansea spent two years as part of his training at its 77 Old Brompton Road shop. He recalls the shop's concave windows with their green and steel surrounds and a big palm house near the

Moyses Stevens first premises was in Victoria Street, in 1876. Many notable florists began their careers as trainees with this famous London firm.

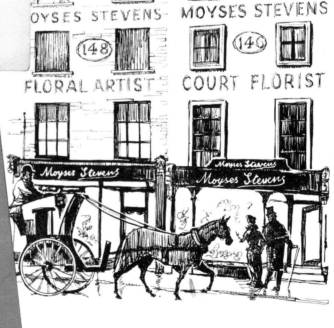

shop in which pots of birds of paradise, *Strelitzia*, really looked as though they were rows of elegant birds about to take flight. Robin's father paid approximately £2 a week for his training.

The practice of paying apprentices went back a long way. Those who learnt floristry by this method generally came from upper- or middle-class backgrounds where there was money to pay for fees. Instead of being an apprentice, a prospective florist could learn by working as a junior in a shop. In 1948 Joan Pearson's stepfather wrote to the firm of Moyses Stevens, asking if there was an opening for seventeen-year-old Joan. Moyses Stevens had started in 1876, with a small shop at 146 Victoria Street run by a Miss Moyses and Mr A.H. Stevens (and was owned by a granddaughter of Miss Moyses up until quite recent times). During the 1930s the Victoria Street shop was made much bigger and another shop opened in Berkeley Square. After an interview Joan went as a junior to the Victoria Street shop. By then the firm boasted of being the largest flower organization in the *world* with a staff of 130. Out of these, there were thirty juniors aged between

Joan Pearson, the talented floral designer who was trained at Moyses Stevens and who has passed on her knowledge to students at evening classes.

fifteen and seventeen years old, each undergoing two and a half to three years of training.

Joan became one of the firm's top floral designers and stayed with them until her retirement. Looking back, she says:

> There were not many flower shops around in those days and the Victoria shop was very impressive. The frontage was Portland marble and there was a big, heavy doorway decorated with polished steel. Inside, it was lit by chandeliers and natural daylight was let in through the roof area from what were known as 'lay' lights. These had Lalique glass in them which had a spider pattern at each corner. The floor was of fine blocks of stone and it was scrubbed every day by ladies on their hands and knees.
>
> In the left-hand window there were cut flowers and a large blackboard

The impressive interior of the Moyses Stevens shop in Berkeley Square.

on which were wreaths made in twelve or thirteen designs. Round about 1951, the price for a wreath was one guinea (that was rock bottom); upwards to one pound, ten shillings; then two pounds; through to fifteen pounds; and twenty pounds. Some special ones could be fifty pounds or seventy pounds. A customer would come in and say, 'I want a wreath so and so …' and I'd do a quick calculation and they'd say, 'Don't be so foolish', because we quoted high figures, but a seventy pound cross could be five feet long. Some of the window display wreaths had a fringe of snow-drops and muscari [grape hyacinths] all round them and each flower had to be wired. These were the more expensive ones. The area inside the right-hand window was tiled with shiny black tiles and on these were baskets of flowers, vases of flowers, little things and bigger baskets.

At that time the flowers in the window were kept cool in summer by

water running down the windows from minute pinholes. It came down in waves and made the view of the windows slightly fuzzy. Sometimes a hole bunged up and had to be cleared, or there was a gap. The girls hated it because it became so damp inside.

A senior girl would have two juniors, and promotion only came when someone left. Mossing was a first job for juniors and you might start preparation work for the wreath, wiring; the senior girl put it together. When I started Miss Phillips was a senior. She'd paid ten shillings a week to go there as an apprentice. After the war she went on the *Queen Mary* to New York to do the wreaths representing Britain at the peacetime celebrations. I learnt from Miss Phillips and Miss Fairbrother, who had also been taught by Miss Phillips. Her work was very delicate. She was known as 'Fairy'; her aunt, sister and cousin also worked there.

Harold Stevens, the son of the shop's founders, Miss Moyses and Mr Stevens, was the owner and wore a bowler hat – so he was known as 'Bowler Hat'. His son-in-law, Phil Houlbrooke, took over from him for a while. Then Mr Stevens's daughter took charge of the business. She was, of course, the granddaughter of the founders. Mr Stevens was the buyer and when he went to market Miss Adams went with him and she then became the buyer. You told Miss Adams what was wanted and she'd go up to the market at 5.00 a.m., or earlier. Flowers were seasonal then. For example, you never had roses in winter and carnations would die in fog.

She brought the flowers back with her in their wooden boxes about 6.30 a.m. or 7.00 a.m. and unpacked. Gardenias came eighteen to a box, each wrapped in cotton wool; thruppence a bloom was rock-bottom price for them. You'd use five or so for a bowl arrangement. We had cabinets like big fridges in which to put the flowers. You could walk into the cabinets – they had doors two arms' width wide. They were kept at about forty degrees Fahrenheit. It was difficult to keep the flowers in the actual shop cool in hot and humid weather and at such times we took the glass out of the front doors. They had been designed to be removable.

In the winter, the workroom, which was on the same floor as the shop, was freezing and we weren't allowed to wear boots. We'd look forward to a warm cup of tea but I remember that one day when it was brought down to us it was blue. You see, we sometimes used to dye flowers with a fine powder and when one of the girls was coming down from a kind of gallery place she'd fallen over and spilt this blue powder which had lingered in the air and turned our tea blue!

Discipline was so strict that it was almost like a prison camp but at the end of the day we weren't any the worse for it. Start time was 8.30 a.m. but that was the time you had to be on the shop floor with your overalls on, not the time you came into the building. Finishing time was 5.30 p.m. We also worked on Saturdays until one o'clock but in busy periods we might work all day, often with a 7.00 a.m. start. There was a clocking-on machine which we had to put our card into, negotiating the great big wooden flower boxes waiting to go back to market. We clocked out in our overalls, so we put hats and coats on afterwards. In a whole week you were allowed only ten minutes' lateness, morning and lunchtimes, and sometimes you couldn't help being late if your train was held up. After ten minutes' worth you lost any commission you'd earned. Commission was a ha'penny in the pound for juniors, three ha'pence for seniors and three ha'pence for salesgirls. I was fortunate in working on some expensive wreaths but, really, often when your commission arrived at the end of the week it was thruppence!

Going back to strictness, my sister planned to get married on a Saturday morning and I had to ask Mr Stevens for the time off and I remember that he said, 'I'll let you know on that Friday' – or something similar! However, sometimes he'd treat a group of staff by taking them to Fuller's, the famous restaurant and tea house. I can remember the lightness of their cakes and the tea in a silver teapot.

Berkeley Square was the posh shop. It was mostly staffed by titled debs and it even had a visitors' book. There was a big artist's board there filled with corsages. Some were cattleya orchids. The corsages were bought and given as luxury gifts, particularly just after the war when there were no chocolates around. There were also white or clove carnation buttonholes for sale. The work for the making up of these items was mostly done in the shop in Victoria. I remember that we used to make the millionaire Gorbenken an orchid buttonhole every day. The flower was sent by orchid growers and it would be collected at the station parcels office but sometimes, if there was a rush on, collection was actually off the platform. Mr Gorbenken's chauffeur would call to pick up the finished buttonhole and his uniform always matched the colour of the car he was driving!

We also did corsages and other gift flowers to be delivered to the Golden Arrow. The train had Pullman carriages and went on the first leg of the journey to Paris from Platform Nine at Victoria station. One of the delivery men took the corsage to the station in a cellophane box and looked for the person who was to receive it on the train.

Girls used to have their own customers for years and knew what they liked. On one occasion a customer got a different assistant but the normal assistant found out and managed to save a potentially embarrassing situation. For example, you had to be extremely careful about cards, particularly for gentlemen who used to send flowers to various ladies; the right message had to go on each!

Do you know, the whole world came through that door, from market traders' daughters to lords and ladies – people you'd never meet anywhere else!

Joan did not only meet the rich and famous at the shop; she had not been with the firm long before she was taken out by senior staff to decorate various premises.

When the Queen was still Princess Elizabeth we went to Clarence House twice a week. I can remember Prince Charles when he was a very little boy offering us a piece of fudge. I also used to help decorate for banquets at Buckingham Palace. The gold plate on the table looked lovely and the distance between place settings was measured. When the Queen came to inspect people melted away, but on one occasion I remained behind with Mrs Howard Stevens and was presented to the Queen. We also decorated the sides of the ballroom.

Another contract was to decorate William Kent's casino where Lord Lucan gambled. It was close to the shop. We'd do the bar, the main gaming room and the reception. The surroundings were very luxurious – like being in heaven. I've also decorated churches and synagogues, and done arrangements for Asprey's, if they had a special item they wanted to show off with flowers. I remember, too, that Sotheby's came round with a big silver wine cooler which they'd sold and we were asked to put flowers in it for the purchaser. Similarly, H. R. Owen's, the car dealers in Berkeley Square, would put a bunch of flowers in all the cars they sold.

As Joan's account suggests, wherever they trained, flower shop juniors, girls or boys (but juniors were usually girls) coming into their jobs straight from school, found that working in a flower shop was certainly not a bed of roses. As late as 1960 a florists' manual advised employers to make sure applying

WREATHS. BOUQUETS. CROSSES.

Case Bros

The staff of Case Bros, Cardiff in the 1930s.

juniors did not have a weak heart or rheumatism. Indeed, an ideal candidate should be 'healthy; strong; have the ability to resist colds; and possess strong feet and legs'.

Comments from those who recall the 1940s and 1950s shops further illustrate how demanding the work was: 'Work rooms looked horrendous and they were so cold. I remember the door frozen to the step at Gough's at Bedford, awful cold and an outside loo on which the roof slates leaked.' Prue Headey of Hertfordshire; 'The shops had hardly any heat. In fact they would be kept as cold as possible. This went on until 1964 when the government brought in regulations about the minimum heating temperature in shops for staff. After that there would be perhaps a small heater which staff could get round at teatime.' Waynman Strike of Cleveland; 'The shop had an old block wooden floor which used to get wet. The place was cold and the loos were awful.' Maureen Edwards of Birmingham; 'Flower shops were dull, damp, with no heating and often a concrete floor, usually painted. Girls had cracked hands; tinned buckets were heavy to carry and the wooden flower crates were also heavy. They were strengthened with wire which snapped away from the side of the box and ripped girls' rayon overalls. The overalls (girls generally had two) had to be scrubbed to be kept clean and maybe their mothers only had basic laundry facilities.' Robin Wayne of Swansea. Some florists, however, worried more about the life expectancy of their flowers than the comfort of their staff, and argued that their workrooms came under the Factories Act and thus didn't have to comply with the heating regulations.

Working hours could be long and wages not high. Joan Corles of Birmingham remembers that: 'Before the war all shops opened until 7.00 p.m. I believe it was the wartime black-out which started the 5.00 or 5.30 p.m. closing time. I think I earned seven shillings and sixpence a week when I started at Hector's in Birmingham in 1937.'

Another 1930s junior was Edith Richardson of Newcastle upon Tyne. Edith started work in 1935 aged fourteen at Miss Sarah Gaskin's flower shop, 12 and 13 Grainger Arcade (a city-centre covered market):

> My friend and I started work on the same day. We each got two shillings and sixpence a week and the hours were 7.30 a.m. to 7.00 p.m., and 7.00 a.m. until 10.00 p.m. on Fridays and Saturdays. There were no holidays but half day was Wednesday and we didn't work on Sundays.
>
> I was living with my grandparents at Dentonburn and my friend lived nearby. We walked to and from work but after a while my friend decided to leave the job because the walking, which was four or five miles each way, was too much for her. Sometimes Miss Gaskin would give me tuppence for the bus fare home at night and, if I'd been working hard, she'd give me a shilling extra in my wage.

The Gaskin family had been florists in the market since the turn of the century and when Edith joined the shop, Miss Gaskin employed about twenty-five other staff. Miss Gaskin was obviously a person of character – Edith describes her:

> She was a well-made woman. She dressed in a smart, navy-blue suit and always wore a big hat. She wasn't a practising florist and couldn't even make up a buttonhole. I learnt floristry work from her nephew who worked there and he'd learnt from his mother and father. He also did the buying.
>
> Miss Gaskin had a chauffeur who brought her down from her home in Whitley Bay each day and took her back. Occasionally, I'd go home with her to act as house parlour maid. She had paying guests who I think paid seven shillings and sixpence for lodging. My maid's uniform in the morn-

Grainger Arcade, a covered market in Newcastle.

ing was a navy-blue outfit. In the afternoon I wore a white apron, a cap and plastic cuffs and had to serve high tea to the borders.

Back at the flower shop, one of my jobs was being a 'messenger girl' delivering flowers. I'd usually walk or, if it was too far, be given a couple of pence for the tram or bus.

Edith's job certainly seems to have had variety but for most flower shop juniors, particularly in later years, their routine had a dreary monotony. It was usually sweeping, greening, mossing and perhaps feeding the cat. Sweeping was to keep the place tidy; mossing meant tying handfuls of damp moss tightly on to a wreath frame with string – an unpleasant job in cold weather; and greening was preparing small bunches of foliage such as cupressus and securing it to cover the mossed frame. Greening and mossing were involved in preparing wreath frames ready for one of the make-up staff to furnish with flowers.

Occasionally an older member of staff might show a junior how to wire flowers and encourage them to make a buttonhole or corsage, but the novice was expected to take their effort to pieces afterwards and straighten the wires for reuse, as most employers were conscious of the old trade maxim, 'A florist's profits are found in his wastebin.'

Janet Carter of Oxford remembers her father Joe Austin's strictness over economy in the 1950s at their shop in St Aldate's:

> Dad was careful about using everything we could. We'd leave buds until they came out, although he used to think buds as beautiful as flowers. Sometimes he'd say to me, 'There's sixpence on the floor there.' It would be a wire which had dropped. Of course it wasn't worth sixpence but what he meant was that it was worth money and to pick it up.
>
> We used silver sand for years in which to set arrangements. We had a bag of it from the builders' yard and tipped back in what hadn't been sold. Also, if a piece of work wasn't sold I'd have to unpick it so that we could reuse the wires and moss. It was hard on your hands and they got ingrained with soil and stained green from most jobs. Some people would get dermatitis on their hands from working with flowers such as daffs or tulips, and I know someone who had an allergy to chrysanthemums.

Joe Austin was a stickler for hard work. He walked on crutches, having had a bicycling accident when he was a boy, and had part of his leg amputated. During the ensuing years he suffered much ill-health and eventually had to have his whole leg removed. Despite this he always worked hard. Janet recalls:

> We lived above the shop, and I can remember that although he was very ill he used to sit up in bed and make wreaths and when I started working in the shop he'd never allow me to be idle. He'd say: 'You got nothing to do? Well, start that wiring or mossing . . . or clean those buckets.' We worked every spare second and always had to have a supply of wreath bases in case someone wanted a wreath at short notice, because you never said 'No' to an order.

By the 1930s there was another route to floristry, other than starting as a lowly junior or being a paying apprentice (the practice of which ceased around the late 1950s). This was to go to a floristry school. However, such places were rare. Bob Fowler believes that for many years there were only two such schools, one in Glasgow – this was probably the Glasgow School of Floristry in Great Western Road – and one in London, Silvester's School of Floral Art run by Mr Jolis in Baker Street. Several retired florists recall having been taught well at Silvester's. Gwen Pickard, who believes that the school closed at the beginning of the Second World War, remembers Mr Jolis as being 'a wizard with his hands', even if they were rather sausage-like rather than taperingly artistic; and another ex-pupil was impressed with her thorough training.

The person who had the most widespread influence in the training of florists both in a shop and at a training school, as well as fame in floral decoration, was undoubtedly Constance Spry. She was born in Derby in 1886 and in 1901 her parents settled in Dublin. She became a health lecturer and married. However, she parted from her husband and took a welfare job in England, bringing her small son Edward with her. Eventually, in 1921 she became the principal of Homerton & South Hackney Day Continuation School in London's East End and married Henry Spry.

Constance enjoyed doing flower arrangements for her friends. Her style was original. It bore no resemblance to the dome-shaped arrangement which lingered on as a legacy from Victorian times. She also often used flowers and foliage not normally associated with flower arranging and mixed wild flowers with cultivated ones.

In 1928, one of her friends introduced her to cinema magnate Sidney Bernstein, who asked her to decorate the foyers of his cinemas. In 1929, she had her first shop in Pimlico, behind Victoria station. She later wrote: 'When … I opened a flower shop it was with far too little knowledge either of conditions or techniques. For example, I did not realize then that arranging flowers in the ordinary sense of the word was not part of a florist's job.' Her inexperience must have showed in other ways too, for when she first went to buy flowers at Covent Garden market one of the salesmen 'gave her a fortnight'.

Of course, Constance was to prove this prophecy gloriously incorrect. Her stepping stone to future fame was an introduction to stage designer Norman Wilkinson, who was redesigning Atkinson's, the perfume shop in Old Bond Street. He asked Constance to undertake flower decorations there to complement his work. She did and so many people came to gaze in the window at them that traffic was stopped and police had to organize crowd control.

She moved her shop to Burlington Gardens and in 1934 she moved again, taking a lease on 64 South Audley Street and also opening a flower arranging school and a shop in Marsham Street, Pimlico. At this time she was doing flowers for the Prince of Wales (who later became Edward VIII) at St James's Palace. The following tale is among archival papers relating to Constance, now held in the Royal Horticultural Society library. Constance had told it to a friend who had made a gaffe, to make her feel better. It was repeated by the friend thus:

As a rule everything [at St James's Palace] was left to her. But one day someone on the telephone had given her precise instructions about the flowers for that evening. This was so unusual that Connie rang St James's Palace, asking for the Comptroller, and said, 'Look, have you by any chance got a new housekeeper called Mrs Simpson?' There was a long gap and then he said, 'Mrs Spry, any orders that come from St James's Palace from Mrs Simpson should be instantly complied with.'

In 1937, Constance went to France to decorate the Château de Condé for the wedding of the Duke of Windsor (as Edward VIII became after he abdicated) and Mrs Simpson.

In May 1946, she began a new venture, the Constance Spry Flower School. Fred Wilkinson, now principal of the school, near Farnham, Surrey, explains:

Her friend Rosemary Hume had a cookery school, and they talked of joining up, having flowers and cookery taught in one place because after the war houses didn't have cooks and so it was a good time to train girls. Constance was reading *Country Life* in bed one night and saw a photo of Winkfield House, near Windsor, and said to her husband, 'I think it'll do.' Her husband said, 'Go ahead'; that was in May 1946 and the school opened at Winkfield in September 1946.

It was the time of rationing. The students made hand-made wallpaper. She bought some bolts of bright yellow felt and put it down as carpet in what became known as the Yellow Drawing Room. She also bought some parachute silk for curtain making and dyed it pink. When she moved to Winkfield, Constance brought flowers from her previous home and although the garden was full of couch, there wasn't time to weed it and the flowers were put straight in. This proved a problem later but she would never allow weedkillers. Once some was put down but it rained, causing it to run and kill plants, and weedkillers were banned from then on!

An assistant wraps flowers among the impressive decor of Constance Spry's South Audley Street shop.

The year 1947 saw Constance Spry and her decorating team working on flowers in Westminster Abbey for the wedding of Princess Elizabeth and Lieutenant Philip Mountbatten. In 1953, at the request of the Minister of Works, she executed floral decorations inside and outside Westminster Abbey for the coronation. She also decorated Westminster Hall where a luncheon was to be given to the Queen's guests. She was awarded an OBE for this work.

Constance died of a stroke on 3 January 1960, aged seventy-three. Two lorries and a van carried hundreds of wreaths to her funeral.

Constance Spry.

One lady who trained under and worked closely with Constance Spry was Sheila Macqueen. Sheila was to become one of Britain's most famous flower arrangers, but all she knew in 1933 was that after leaving school she wanted to work with flowers. Looking back to that time she says:

My family were sympathetic to the idea. My mother and grandmother were great gardeners and my father was artistic. My sister painted and went to the Slade.

I went with my mother to the London School of Floristry in the basement of Daniel Neale's shop in Bond Street. By the side of the steps leading down to the school there was a violin stand and on it a white bouquet. I said to my mother, 'Before we go any further I don't want to learn anything about that sort of triangular bouquet!' Mother said, 'Let's go down to Bond Street and look in Atkinson's, the perfume shop, because they always have the most wonderful flower decorations.' So we went and saw there a brown ceramic vase which was reputed to have come from the tomb of Tutankhamun and it was filled with old man's beard and sprays of berries. We walked into the shop and there was a Miss Phillips in charge and she told us that the flowers were done by a flower shop in nearby Burlington Gardens. So we went off to find the shop. It was called Flower Decorations Ltd, and was owned by Mrs Constance Spry. I was interviewed by Eleanor Gilbert, Mrs Spry's secretary, who said, 'We've got one pupil, but if she leaves, we'll contact you.' Of course I prayed that she'd leave. She did, and aged nineteen I started as a paying pupil – Father paid the premium.

The other staff were: Beryl, a cockney who lived in the East End and who was a fully qualified florist and who made the wreaths and bouquets; a buyer named George Foss; Miss Oldfield who ran the shop – she was a good florist and kept calm, never getting in a flap; Val Pirie, who did decorating; and the senior decorator Joyce Robinson, who was known as 'Robo' – I learnt more from her than from anyone. Mrs Spry was there one minute and gone the next. Robo worked for the Mountbattens at Broadlands in their garden and doing their house decorations in the summer and came to us in winter; then she came full-time.

One of my first jobs was dethorning roses with a pair of scissors – a terrific job because we had boxes of 'em. I remember that I was given a branch of sloes and Mrs Spry said, 'Strip that.' I didn't know what strip meant but one of the others told me that it was to take the leaves off and just leave the berries. I started the job and Mrs Spry came by and said, 'If there are no berries on a branch don't bother stripping it!' I'd been stripping berryless branches and just leaving a bare stem.

We wore white, thick, linen overalls, knee-length, with huge pockets for scissors – just like coats. The linen was coarse so the overalls practically stood up by themselves. They were specially made. We wore our overalls if we went to do decorating at say, the Savoy, but if we were doing other contract work, we wore ordinary clothes.

I went out to help decorate more or less straight away. In fact the following Monday I went to help with Atkinson's window. It was my second week and Mrs Spry did half a vase and left me to finish it. Atkinson's was done every day and other floral contract work was at Elizabeth Arden and Cyclax, both opposite us in Bond Street.

Constance Spry wasn't really famous at that time. We started on a shoestring. Not long ago I said to Eleanor Gielgud, who had worked there too, that I always remembered going to Covent Garden with big wooden boxes which were chargeable and we had to get money back before we could buy flowers! There was no capital.

Mrs Spry's first shop had been in Belgravia Square just by Eccleston Bridge. She used to bring stuff up from the country that she had grown at her home, Parkgate at Chelsfield near Orpington, Kent – paeonies and lovely old roses – but, of course, a lot of times there

One of Constance Spry's most famous pupils, Sheila Macqueen.

wasn't anything in the garden to bring up so she had to buy at Covent Garden and because you had to buy in dozen or half-dozen bunches, she had to start a shop to sell what she couldn't use herself. In addition to market flowers Lady Loader used to come up in her little van from Nyman's and Leonard's Lee and bring bunches of rhododendrons and azaleas which she sold to us. They were only prunings. There was also a private garden in Cornwall which used to send up camellias.

Flowers were put in buckets out on the pavement; there was no shop window – in fact it was virtually just a little house. Then she moved to Burlington Gardens which was a shop, a nice shop, and good for a florist because it had a basement with tunnels where flowers could be kept cool. I remember that there was an old log like a tree trunk with a mallet tied on to it with a piece of string and we used to use this to crush stems before putting the stock in water.

Constance Spry's business seemed to build up from the moment I got there. Suddenly she was getting known. She knew Lady Portarlington from the days when she'd lived in Ireland and she started doing flowers for her in Grosvenor Square. The Duke of Kent went to lunch and admired the flowers there, and then of course we got asked to do his flowers too. By this time, 1934, we had moved to the shop in South Audley Street, which had huge cellars with arched domed roofs which went under the road. We'd started off with only about seven of us but within eighteen months there was a staff of about seventy! It just grew like Topsy.

Mrs Spry was very clever in the way she decorated the window of the South Audley Street shop. She bought yards and yards of white surgical sheeting and we pleated it and made screens which divided the shop from the window, for it was all one room. We put a raised platform in the window. We had some brown ceramic vases, two-handled, about eighteen inches high – I believe they'd been kilned in Cornwall. We painted them white and they went onto the platform which was about one and a half feet high. Then we had some white stands at various heights. In the vases were bunches for sale or single flowers. If it was carnations there was a whole mass. Everything looked meticulous; there was never a spot of water or dead leaf – Miss Oldfield saw to that. After we'd been in South Audley Street for about two years she retired; she was a wonderful person.

Miss Standfast, an old schoolfriend of Mrs Spry's, had the art department above the shop and made artificial flowers.

Eventually I was given five shillings a week wage and this went on for some time; then I got a rise, but the following week it was taken off because they couldn't afford to pay it to me!

I used to get in to the shop about 8.15 a.m. and often never got home until eight or nine o'clock at night. For instance, if there was a coming-out ball Mrs Spry insisted we hand the girl her bouquet just before she left for the ball. I'd get a taxi at eight o'clock at night and go into the hall, and the girl would be there with feathers in her hair and I'd hand her the bouquet. The débutantes used to bring in a piece of their dress material when they ordered a bouquet.

At lunchtimes a boy used to come round with a box on a bike and he sold sixpenny snacks called 'tikky snacks'. They were sandwiches, a pie or a cheese roll. At first anyone made the tea at elevenses and teatime, and then a girl that came did it. Mrs Spry would buy us all cakes from Fortnum's if we were working late – walnut, iced cakes which we ate with our filthy hands.

I just loved flower arranging. I was no good at making wreaths, although we did have to try to learn. Mrs Ernest Simpson was on my contract. She had a flat in Eaton Square. When she became more involved with Edward VIII they had a house, Fort Belvedere, at Windsor, and we decorated that too. It was a pretty house with a lovely drawing room. It was built in turrets and had circular windows. We used to put masses of daffs and catkins in horrible glass tanks which had once been used to hold battery accumulators.

The second time we went to Fort Belvedere the King invited Mrs Spry to lunch with him. I was decorating with Mrs Gotto, the second head. He came out of the dining room to ask if we'd eaten. I said, 'No'. He went back into the dining room and cut some ham and put it between slices of bread and brought it out to us. Mrs Gotto said, 'I never thought I'd see the day when the king of England got me a ham sandwich. If I wasn't so hungry I'd take it home and press it in the Bible!'

When we went out decorating we usually did all the work on the spot. Mrs Spry insisted we went in the front door and always worked in rooms with dust sheets. I remember that one old boy called us 'Mrs Spry's young ladies'. Very often we'd have a glass of sherry with the butler then be given another upstairs, so pretended we hadn't had one.

Like other top London florists, Constance Spry's shop made débutantes' bouquets. Designs for them varied – here is a fashionable 1930s example.

Once a year I did dried flowers for an elderly lady called Princess Helena-Victoria who lived in St James's. I had tea with her. I don't recall much conversation. Then at other places we'd have tea in the servants' quarters. I remember that at Lady Aberconway's there was an Aubusson carpet which we weren't allowed to walk on. We had to walk all the way round the edge to do the flowers on the mantelpiece and back again.

My mother loved to hear all about it. It was not glamorous, people think it was, but it wasn't.

Whether it was decorating for a party in Brighton or in Leicestershire we always went to look at the place first, although I can't remember our ever overnighting anywhere. I recall on one occasion a huge coming-out do in Hampshire where there was an avenue of limes. We picked the lime which was just coming out into flower, and stripped the leaves because you can't see the flower bracts with them on.

Mrs Spry never 'did' a vase of flowers in front of anybody in her whole life. We were all chucked out. For the illustrations in her books and on calendars she'd pick everything for the photographic day and put it in the bath. Then she'd say, 'Now I want that in that vase,' and I put it in. If she didn't like it she told me what to take out. She knew exactly what she wanted. The fact that she wouldn't arrange in front of people gave me a bonus for when she went to lecture in Australia after the war I went with her to demonstrate.

Sheila went on to help with the floral decorations for royal weddings, including the present Queen's, and also assisted when Constance Spry was asked to do decorations for the Queen's coronation in 1953.

Just before the Second World War Sheila left Constance Spry's to get married but, when her husband was posted to Burma, she went back to the shop and did flowers for special occasions. She explains: 'There was really no one else around to do all the weddings then. Girls had gone to work in munitions factories or were in the forces. I can remember waiting outside churches to collect containers and listening to doodlebugs and sirens.'

Sheila was later awarded an MBE for her work with flowers and became well known in this country and overseas. Recently the gardens of a stately mansion in Virginia, USA, have been dedicated to Sheila. The house at Millwood was left for the enjoyment and education of the American people and a group known as the Sheila Macqueen Flower Ladies designed and maintain the gardens.

❀

CHAPTER FOUR

A changing business – in war and peace

In 1921, H. Stephenson, florist of Old Market Place, Grimsby, received a telegram addressed to 'The Leading Florist, Grimsby'. It requested a floral tribute to be made up and delivered to a lady in Grimsby. Stephenson carried out the order and the lady said that her son in Canada had ordered the flowers and she gave him her son's address to write to. She also said she would tell her son that she had received the flowers. Her son sent Stephenson's letter to the Canadian florist from whom he had requested the flowers and this florist sent payment to Stephenson, enclosing at the same time details of an organization called the FTDA (Florists' Telegraph Delivery Association).

Mr Stephenson was so impressed with the idea of an organization through which orders could be gained from America that he wrote to the FTDA and offered to be its agent in Britain. However, the association wrote back to say it 'thought' that some British florists were thinking of setting up their own branch, so nothing further was done at the time.

The FTDA itself had started about eleven years earlier, almost by accident. No one can recall the exact circumstances but it is believed that a couple of American florists, meeting at a convention of the Society of American Florists, discussed the problems of sending flowers by rail. America being so large and the climatic conditions so varied, any order having spent four days in a box in a rail goods wagon inevitably arrived the worse for wear. To overcome this problem the two florists agreed that if one received an order to go to someone in the other's area, he would telegraph the order to the other. The other would make up the flowers, deliver them fresh, and they would settle up the money between them. The plan worked and in 1909 nine American florists met in Rochester to discuss setting up an organization to further the idea. This was the Florists' Telegraph Delivery Association, which formally started in 1910.

After a few years the horticultural trade press in Britain began to write about the FTDA and some British florists joined it as 'foreign' members, including Joe Dobson of Leighton's florists in Glasgow, and Carl Engelmann, a nurseryman and

A.J. Fowler
Southampton's
F.T.D Member

carnation grower of Saffron Walden in Essex. Bob Fowler recalls that his father, Arthur, became a member just after the First World War. Almost immediately they started to get 'bon voyage' orders from America.

By 1923 there were seventeen British foreign members of the FTDA. Nine were from London: Carlton White, Felton's, Harrods, Longmans, Moyses Stevens, Piper & Son, Shearn's, Silvester's, and Wills & Segar. The others were Bees Ltd of Liverpool, Cohen's of Birkenhead, Carl Engelmann of Saffron Walden, Fowler's of Southampton, Jameson's of Dublin, Leighton's of Glasgow, Tait and Francis of Edinburgh, and Treseder's of Cardiff.

An editor and managing director of a horticultural publishing company in London, J.S. Brunton, was impressed with the FTDA's activities in America – in 1922 its turnover had been $12 million – and had written articles about it in the *Horticultural Trade Magazine*. In May 1923 he and Carl Engelmann invited all the British foreign members to a meeting at the Wilton Hotel in Victoria, London. Most turned up. They discussed the possible gains to be had from forming their own British unit, and decided to do so. They decided also to publicize themselves in Britain and in the colonies. It was, after all, a novel concept for the public and other florists to grasp, for in no other trade could you buy from a retailer in one city and have delivery made by a retailer in another. By 1939 they had 1,000 members.

In 1946 Southampton florist, Douglas Bailey, suggested that to help deal with overseas orders they adopt a common 'floral' currency. It was called the 'fluerin' and each country's currency was valued against it. For example, in 1947 one fluerin was worth: £1 3d in England; $0.25 in America; 27.50 francs in France; 53.00 lire in Italy; and 60.00 milreis in Palestine.

The fluerin system continues to this day, with its value being worked out for the most part by the movement of sterling against the Swiss franc.

The name 'Interflora' was adopted in 1950 when it was thought an easier title was needed to popularize the association than 'Florists' Telegraph Delivery Association'.

In 1968, the last survivor of the original seventeen florists who had met in 1923 died. He was eighty-one-year-old Sam Segar. Sam had been made Treasurer at that first meeting and continued as such for a record forty-five years!

Of course, the working of a flower relay service was too good an idea to remain the province of one organization. In 1947 three Southampton florists set up their own system, the British Teleflower Service Ltd. And since that date several other relay services have also been developed.

❀

At the outbreak of the Second World War steps had to be taken to increase home food production, for it was known that importing food would be difficult. To this end the Ministry of Agriculture began to issue 'Cropping Orders' to nurserymen and market growers.

Flowers were a luxury crop and the Orders gradually stipulated that their growing, both under glass and in the open ground, should be reduced and be replaced with vegetable and salad crops. For example, glasshouse flower growers had to grow tomatoes in summer and lettuce and cress in winter. By 1942 flower growers were allowed to keep only 10 per cent of their 1939 acreage of flowers. That was just sufficient for them to preserve their stock plants so that when the war ended they could start to rebuild their flower businesses.

Prior to the war, John Godsmark, a Sussex nurseryman, had been growing chrysanthemums and sweet peas. The sweet peas could be sown from seed so there was no storage space needed for preserving them but the chrysanthemums were propagated by cuttings so his 10 per cent of space was taken up with these.

Before the war a special train with goods wagons, arranged through the West Sussex Growers, had transported his flowers to market. He explains: 'The engine came along the line at 5.00 or 6.00 p.m. and called at local stations where growers would be pulled in waiting to load their produce for market. When the train got to Nine Elms in London, Southern Railway men unloaded it and took the boxes on lorries to the wholesalers in old Covent Garden.' But in the last season before the Cropping Orders became severe John had a considerable amount of chrysanthemums ready for market and was faced with a problem of getting them there, for the government had placed restrictions on petrol and from 1 November 1942 there was a ban on transporting flowers by rail. With even a ban on sending flowers by post, it seemed that the growers' crops would waste – but then they had an idea.

'If I tell people about it now they don't believe me,' said John. 'It's a seventy-mile journey from the south coast to Covent Garden market but the plan was to send the flowers on a long four-wheeled cart, like a hay cart, horse-drawn, and change the horse every ten miles or so, or whenever there was a pick-up of flowers – like a stage coach!' And this they did. The system was difficult to run but it kept up long enough for most growers to clear their flower crops. 'We sent chrysanthemums that way for about six weeks of the year.'

It was noted how many people with suitcases began to be seen around the markets. A suitcase could hold small spring flowers and be carried on the train without questions being asked, as it looked like ordinary luggage. Another scheme to beat the rail ban was scooping the hearts out of broccoli, filling the cavities with anemones and carefully covering them with the genuine material. In an ingenious

FLOWER SMUGGLERS PUNISHED

Two London men were sent to jail at Penzance for having unlawfully used petrol in a lorry which the police said contained a hundred and thirty-eight boxes of flowers, costing £150, but worth £2,000 to £3,000 in London.

One man was sentenced to twelve months' imprisonment for misusing petrol, and four months for dangerous driving, both with hard labour, the imprisonment to be concurrent; the other was sentenced to six months' hard labour. It was stated in the course of the case that fifty gallons of petrol would be used by the lorry on the journey to Penzance and back.

The Gardener's Chronicle, 27 March 1943

scam carried out at a West Country railway station, a hearse arrived with a coffin, which was booked on to a London train. However, officials at the station became suspicious because the wreaths accompanying it all had violets as their base instead of the customary moss and fern. This was at a time when a dozen bunches of violets sold in Cornwall for four shillings but in Covent Garden would realize twenty-four shillings. Detectives came to open the coffin and found it full of flowers!

Representations from the flower trade were made to the Minister of Agriculture regarding the rail ban and by April 1942 it was partially lifted. However, nothing could be done about the cut in flower growing and any stock to supplement supplies was sought. Katherine Sloan, from Newcastle, the fourth generation of her family to be involved in flower selling (her daughter is the fifth), remembers as a little girl in the war years walking with her grandmother, mother and helpers out into the countryside each February to pick snowdrops:

We'd get permission to go into woods and pick as many as ten pillowcase-fuls. We'd also pick boxwood from tall trees. The snowdrops were brought back home and bunched by the family (everyone participating) into twenty-four snowdrops a bunch with an ivy leaf wrapped round and tied with thread. They were sold to market the next day, about twenty dozen, at, I believe, thruppence a bunch.

Edith Richardson, who was a florist in Grainger Arcade (a large indoor market in the centre of Newcastle) all her working life and worked in the 1970s with Katherine in Katherine's first shop there, remarked: 'You had to have delicate hands to bunch the fragile stems of snowdrops and primroses the same.' Edith herself never picked wildflowers but supplemented wartime stocks with her cleverly formed artificial flowers made with crêpe paper and rhododendron foliage.

Janet Carter explained how the war affected her father's florist's shop in Oxford: 'There were very few flowers but enough to get by with. There might have been a bit of lilac about you could put in. Wreaths were mostly foliage. All the florists' deliveries had to be pooled. There was a flower shop owner called Joe Brown, and his son was responsible for doing all the local deliveries for florists.'

Mrs Ellen Johnson, a member of the Costello family (an old, established florists of Newcastle), waits patiently beside her flower barrow. The Costellos picked snow-drops during the war years to supplement their meagre flower supplies.

Mrs Green outside the Colleen Bawn pub.

Bob Fowler of Southampton also recalls how wartime wreaths were more greenery than flowers: 'We used to do chaplets with cycas leaves and put a spray on the bottom. It took fewer flowers.' Christine Hinds (née Green) of Bermondsey remembers her mother's unique wartime wreaths: 'She'd open a big tulip flat, it might have been four or six inches in diameter, and attach it on to a mossed ring and green it with cupresses.'

She also describes the bombing that affected so many florists:

> Mum – who was taught to be a florist by my father's granny, Louise Harris – had a stall on the forecourt of a pub called the Colleen Bawn on the corner of Old Collingbourne Road. One night the pub was bombed and from then on Mum had to move her pitch out more into the road. Our family – my father James Frederick Green was a florist too – also had a tiny shop in Peckham Park Road and that was bombed in 1942. There was a body in the doorway the next morning. We got a shop in St James's Road near enough opposite and I was born above that in 1944.

In London's West End, Goodyear's was also bombed. Derek Goodyear, who had been drafted into the services as a gunner during the war years recalls:

> Our shop was in the 'Royal' Arcade, which was called that because the royal shirt maker was there and the royal florist (ourselves). The arcade was between Albermarle Street and Bond Street. The bomb fell on Gieves, the naval outfitters, but severely damaged our shop. Father, who was also in the Army, happened to be on leave and turned up at the shop that morning to find it bombed. We moved to Brook Street near Claridge's hotel.
>
> During the war the flower trade was poor, although famous people like Herbert Wilcox and Ralph Richardson used to buy a lot of flowers to send to ladies! We mostly sold flowers which had been grown outside and a lot of green plants. Transport was difficult too – we had a horse and cart for deliveries.

One Friday evening in 1940 Mr C.V. Tomlinson, who had a florist's shop in Shirley Road, Southampton, finished preparing a bride's bouquet and placed it ready for collection for a wedding the following day, before shutting up his shop. That night the shop was bombed. The engaged couple had to be told their bouquet was beneath the rubble. However, in order not to let them down Mr Tomlinson gave them a few sprays of freesias which he had managed to get.

On their wedding anniversary the young husband came to Mr Tomlinson, whose shop was now in another road, and asked for a bunch of freesias for his wife. The next year he did the same and this custom went on even after Mr and Mrs Tomlinson's deaths in the 1970s and the passing of the business to Gordon Price. Mr Price, who told me this story, still supplies the freesias.

Bob Fowler's Southampton shop also suffered war damage:

> We lost windows. We were fortunate one time. The two floors above the shop we let to people and in the top one were two girls from the fire service and when an incendiary got in through the roof they got up through the trap door and got it into a bucket, and stopped the shop burning down!
>
> Another time we were in a top flat in the main part of the city and an incendiary dropped through the roof. We were in an air raid shelter at the time. My daughter Jill had left clothes on the settee and the incendiary ignited one of her woollen socks which threw sparks as it rolled onto the floor. The sparks burnt the front off the piano – in fact it's the very piano

Diana has in this room now – we had it restored under war damage. The chap who did the restoration asked me what make it was, I said I didn't have a clue so he said 'Oh, we'll call it "Regent"!'… And you see, that's what we put on it.

I asked Bob what happened to the stock when the windows were blown out.

We used to take stuff out at night. In the end we had steel shutters because they also helped with the blackout where you mustn't show a light at night. In the shop we had a shoe box and made a hole in the top of it and a little slit in the side. We threaded the light cable through the hole in the top and screwed in the bulb then put the lid on the box and there was just enough light coming through the slit to see to take an order from a customer. A lot of businesses closed up early in winter.

The flower-sellers' window from St Clement Dane's church in London.

In May 1941 an incendiary bomb hit St Clement Danes church near London's Covent Garden. After the ensuing fire only the walls and steeple were left standing. Among its treasures destroyed were three items very near to the hearts of London's street flower sellers. The first was a flower basket which had belonged to a woman called Fannie, who had sold flowers from it for over thirty years on Ludgate Hill and had become one of the most famous figures in London. Near the basket had been the second object – a war shrine presented to the church by the 'Flower Sellers'. The shrine, unveiled by Princess Beatrice in 1917, had been an eleven-foot-high cross with, on one side, an angel offering a laurel wreath and, on the other, the parish emblem of the anchor (St Clement had been martyred by being tied to an anchor and thrown in the sea). The third item was a window of stained glass dedicated to the flower sellers and based on the theme of 'I am the rose of Sharon'.

London flower girls.

The flower sellers' window had been designed by the Rector of St Clement Danes, William Pennington-Bickford, and his wife Louie. Of the couple, it was Louie who had the strong link with London's flower girls. Her father, the Reverend Septimus Pennington, had become rector of the church in 1889 and Louie became a special friend and guide to all the street flower sellers who plied their trade with flowers from nearby Covent Garden and Clare markets. She founded a Flower Sellers' Guild in the 1890s and its members were known locally as 'Louie Pennington-Bickford's Flower Girls'. Peter Maplestone, a local historian of the parish of St Clement Danes, writes:

> Although not directly a religious guild, the flower sellers attended regular services at St Clement's and provided a 'guard of honour' at special occasions there. A sort of uniform of identical aprons was instituted and the flower sellers were lined up with their baskets on either side of the entrance.

In 1907 Louie married her father's curate, William Bickford. He became rector when Louie's father died in 1910. The couple were devoted to the church and even wrote their own hymns – William composing the music and Louie the words.

It is said that when the church was bombed in May 1941, William was heartbroken. He died the following month. Louie died on 5 September of the same year.

Her funeral service was held in the ruins of the church. There were a number of flower girls in the congregation. In her will, Louie provided for a fund to be set up for the flower girls. Mr Maplestone tells me that it has only recently been dissolved.

In 1958 the church was rebuilt and the flower girls put a large vase in the entrance in memory of Mrs Pennington-Bickford. The vase also acted as a money box. In the flat tops of its handles were slots in which flower girls could put coins which rolled down and collected in the base of its stand. This money went towards flower decorations for the church. Although still at the church, the vase is no longer in use. Ken Allen, who spent twenty-five years as verger, says that the last time an elderly flower girl dropped a fifty pence piece in it, was fifteen years ago.

As well as destroying buildings in their vicinity, bombing raids during the war had a depressing effect on Covent Garden market. Prior to them, wartime trade had fallen away to nothing – increasingly the scarcity of flowers in the principal markets forced the prices up to undreamed of heights – but was just picking up again when the blitzes started. To comply with blackout regulations the great glass roof of the flower market had to have black curtaining fixed inside it and the doors had to be masked. This allowed trade to continue. Some wholesalers, like John Collingridge Ltd, moved their business to the market cellars.

With wood and cardboard on ration, wholesalers put out a plea to florists to return all their empty boxes promptly. The problem of lack of packing materials was so great that at one point experiments were carried out to see if flower boxes could be made of aluminium. Whether this aluminium was to be from the great piles of pots and pans collected to be recycled for plane building, and, it is believed, ultimately not used for that purpose, is not known!

Of course lack of certain materials affected flower shops, too. Florists' wire was virtually unobtainable and wooden picks (like toothpicks) or straightened-out hairpins were used instead. In southern Ireland (where the floristry trade was badly hit by flower supplies being cut off from England and Northern Ireland, and having to rely on exorbitantly priced local supplies), there were reports of enterprising florists making 'stub' wires by cutting up clothes line, old telegraph wire and even reclaimed wire from old motor tyres. Here, too, wooden wreath boxes were becoming very expensive. The cheapest was a twenty-inch one, at 10s but the use of wooden boxes instead of cardboard or leatherboard was often necessary to withstand long train journeys and the handling at customs posts.

In Britain cardboard flower boxes for shop customers were hard to get and in 1941 the government made the problem worse by banning the use of wrapping

paper on all bought articles. It was also difficult to obtain containers in which to sell flower arrangements. Fowler's in Southampton came up with a solution to this problem. Diana Fowler, Bob Fowler's daughter, showed me examples of what they used: a jug and a small pastry mixing bowl. They had bought up a stock of each and could offer the jug in two sizes and three colours – tan, dark green and yellow. Bob pointed out that the handle on the jug made it easy to lift the flower arrangement, adding, 'Of course there weren't so many arrangements then as now.' Diana had some additional information:

Examples of the jug and pastry bowl which Fowler's used for arrangements when wartime stringencies made new flower containers unobtainable.

It was the days before foam blocks to hold flowers had been invented, and we put a piece of bun moss into the container. The only difference between that and modern foam blocks is that if you made a hole in the moss with a flower stem it closed up! Father used to pay rent to the owner of a wood and we'd go and collect the bun moss from beneath the trees. Oddly enough it grew in quite a dry position amongst beech leaves and, unlike other mosses, it never smelt; ordinary sphagnum soon gets smelly.

Flower shops were not all wartime gloom. There was a silver lining and it came via the servicemen's NAAFI. The Women's Voluntary Service ran canteens for the NAAFI at which they not only served tea and buns but also lent a kindly ear to servicemen who wanted a bunch of flowers delivered to their wives or sweethearts on certain anniversaries. The men wrote a note or letter which the WVS kept carefully until the appropriate dates. The WVS then passed the requests for flowers to local flower shops who used the Interflora system to get the bouquets delivered.

Overseas forces stationed in Britain brought their own kind of trade too. 'Being in Grosvenor Square in London,' Sheila Macqueen said, speaking of Constance Spry's shop, 'we did a big trade in corsages for all the girlfriends of the GIs. It kept us going through the war. American headquarters are in Grosvenor Square and we were close, opposite Good's.'

The GIs didn't forget their folks back home either. Bob Fowler remembered:

We sent thousands of Interflora orders to America for birthdays and Christmases. There were several American hospitals in Southampton and we used to take order forms up to them and an Interflora book which listed American and Canadian member florists. You'd ask patients where they came from and they might say, 'Oh, Detroit'; then you'd look up a florist in Detroit and say, 'Do you know so and so?' and they'd say, 'Yeah, that's only just round the corner from us.' We always talked in dollars.

Nationally, overseas orders grew to such an extent, particularly in the last few years of the war, that Interflora set up special offices to handle the business. There was one in Salisbury and one in Dundee. This arrangement also helped with security, for if orders came from centralized sources they didn't give away troop movements. At its busiest the Dundee office had eighteen girls on its staff and during December 1943 one florist channelled approximately 2,000 orders.

At the end of the war florist shop owners whose premises had been damaged by enemy action set about getting their shops rebuilt. This meant negotiating with the War Damage Authority, town planners and post-war building licence officials, and in some cases the many restrictions made this a lengthy process. The upside was that the shop could be reincarnated on 'modern lines' with emphasis on width, light and air. It was thought that some of these rebuilt 'modern premises' of florists in the south of England compared favourably with spacious American florists' shops.

Perhaps the most important effect of the war was that the high prices of cut flowers during the hostilities had put people off buying them. Thus it was generally agreed in the trade that a concentrated effort was needed to make them popular again. Several enterprising individuals came up with possible publicity slogans, one being 'Let's forget austerity and go gay with flowers'. As it happened, though, such rallying cries were not needed. Bob Fowler explained: 'It's surprising how quickly things got going again – it must have been general relief.'

However, an ideal opportunity to promote flowers arose in 1951. A reminder of it recently came to light in the basement of Robin Wayne's florist's shop in Swansea. Wayne's are the oldest established florists in the city and over the years Robin, and his father before him, accumulated and most fortunately kept memorabilia connected with the florist's trade. I was lucky enough to be present when much of this was being sorted out, prior to Robin vacating his shop for new premises. Among the scores of wire wreath foundations in every shape – harps, anchors, crosses, *et al* – being lifted off the walls, there was one that was completely different. Imagine the star of a compass, then for the top north-pointing spoke substitute the profile of a helmeted head and neck; imagine the west- and east-pointing spokes as being the shoulders (albeit rather pointed ones) beneath the head, and the south-pointing spoke as being normal and star-like but its outer tip bisecting a semi-circle hung with a dozen small shapes like wavy flags or sunrays. 'That's a rarity,' Robin said. 'It's the Festival of Britain emblem.' The frame had stout struts at the back, so it was obviously meant for a standing display and no doubt would have been filled with flowers to match the emblem colours. These were red, white and blue for the star, yellow for the half crescent beneath it and red and blue for the flags (or sunrays).

Robin Wayne of Swansea – St Paul's Cathedral (in the background) is one of the fascinating wire foundations he has used and kept for posterity.

The Festival of Britain in 1951 was good for the florists' businesses recovering from the effects of war. These floral arches were part of Covent Garden's decorations for the celebrations.

Whether it had been displayed in the shop window or had been part of the many events countrywide which celebrated the festival is not known.

The Festival of Britain, to commemorate the centenary of the Great Exhibition of 1851, began in May 1951 and continued for five months. During this time there was a noticeable demand for flowers and plants for use in displays and entertainments. The centrepiece of the festival was an exhibition on the South Bank of the River Thames in London celebrating advances in science, art, discovery and design over the past 100 years. Unfortunately no special place was allocated to flowers but this omission was amply remedied by two stunning floral exhibitions in the flower market at Covent Garden. One was held on 12 and 13 June and the other on 11 and 12 September. They were the first flower shows held in the market's 300-year history.

For the June show a floral curtain was constructed near the market entrance. It contained 3,000 to 5,000 salmon-pink and flame gladioli mounted on 650 feet of rope. Inside the market teams of florists decorated fifty-two overhead floral arches and set up a 'florists' avenue' which showed a wide variety of floral art. Specialist flower societies put on displays and there were competitions in flower arranging and floral art for amateurs and professionals.

Wholesalers A. Goodchild of 30 Wellington Street gave over their entire premises (which looked down on the market entrance) as a press office. Special tables and phones were installed for reporters and newsreel crews. The Foreign Secretary, Herbert Morrison, performed the opening ceremony. Outside the market there were basket-carrying races and children's sports. John Collingridge, who was a small boy at the time, remembers taking part in the sports. The showpiece of the September event was a fifty-feet-high Skylon which incorporated a quarter of a million chrysanthemum blooms.

❀

The post-war years saw a surge of interest in flowers, as well as a number of influences from America on floristry. During the war many shops had relied on part-time or unskilled help and no training had been given to young florists. In an endeavour to raise the standard of floristry, Interflora arranged for an American floral designer, Horace Head, to tour Britain during 1946 and give demonstrations to members and their staff. In all, more than 10,000 people attended his 'schools'.

Florists' sundries were also to benefit from America. Bob Fowler recalls that after the war the first waterproof ribbons started to come in from across the Atlantic. Prior to this flower shops had relied on ordinary draper's ribbon. Also, message tags were to become more well known to British florists. Bob had already discovered them. Just prior to the war he had been reading an American florists' magazine and saw an advertisement for small 'enclosure cards' complete with envelopes. These were for written messages which could then be attached to bouquets, arrangements or funeral tributes. At that time there were very few British florists who would have thought of ordering direct from an American company and dealing in dollars, but Bob saw no difficulty. He contacted the firm, the John Henry Company of Lansing, Michigan, and became probably one of the first florists in Britain to obtain and use florists' 'tag' cards.

There is an interesting story attached to how the cards, so standard today, came to be invented in America. In 1909, two brothers, Henry and William Dudley, went to Lansing and set up a firm called the Dudley Paper Co. Apparently Henry Dudley regularly bought his wife bunches of flowers and liked to write a message to go with them. However, after buying the flowers he found it irksome to have to go to another store to get the card, so in 1912 he bought, perhaps from a drug store, some small 'pill' envelopes and in his attic set about cutting and printing cards to fit the envelopes.

He made enough to be able to offer supplies to local florists. They bought the cards and soon florists from all over Michigan were requesting them. He was also asked if he had other stationery useful to florists, so he printed a selection.

Business was such that Henry Dudley found he could set up a company on his own. His son, John Henry Dudley had been born that year so he called the new enterprise the John Henry Company. By the time John Henry was old enough to call on florists to get their orders the business was in large premises with several presses and staff to cope with orders. The firm continues in Lansing to this day. Martha J. Keeler, the Director of Communications, says of the 'enclosure cards' that, 'The idea for making them was never patented and other printing companies picked it up, but for a long time we didn't have much competition. During our early years we also made the first "care tags" for flowering plants.'

After the war, house plants came into their own. A hint of their emerging popularity was given in an article that appeared in the *Nurseryman and Seedsman* in 1949, written by an American grower whose aim was to kindly alert British nurserymen to a new market which they might cash in on:

> A man came to see me recently to discuss the question of propagating philodendron for him. He told me that his monthly requirements were from three to four million rooted cuttings of this plant, all of which he used for the planting of pots, bowls, hanging ornaments and similar items sold for the decoration of the home … He went on further to say that rooted cuttings of the common English ivy, *Hedera helix*, were used in only slightly less quantities and in America he had great difficulty in obtaining the amount he needed. I have seen from personal observation the quantities of plants of ivy which are used in American homes and strange as it may seem, I believe that in this item there is a real potential for exporting …

Someone, however, was 'ahead of the game' on this score in England, growing pot plants not for exporting to America, but for the home market. That person was Thomas Rochford, a third-generation grower of Turnford Hall Nurseries, Broxbourne, Hertfordshire. In 1947 George Foss, who worked with Constance Spry as her business manager, had shown Rochford nine pots of indoor ivies and cissus which Mrs Spry had brought back from America. He asked if the nursery could take cuttings from the pots and grow on a couple of dozen of each for her as she was 'anxious to get a source of different materials and leaf textures'.

Thomas Rochford obliged and supplied Mrs Spry with regular consignments. Soon other customers wanted them too. Turnford Hall began to turn more and more of the nursery over to green plants. Thomas Rochford also revived interest in beautiful foliaged plants such as dracænas and caladiums.

These plants had enjoyed a vogue in Victorian times. One of their pioneers was gardener-turned-writer Donald Beaton, who in 1838 exhibited at a London flower show a 'collection of rare, curious and fine leaved plants'. There were 425 in all and they were in a special tent set apart from other exhibits because of their unusualness and the 'questionable folly' of exhibiting them. Nevertheless, using fine-leaved plants as decoration became popular and in 1870 a wonderfully illustrated book called *New and Rare Beautiful-leaved Plants*, quite the coffee-table book of its day, was published.

During Edwardian times interest in fine-foliaged plants faded and pot plants with bright flowers, for example azaleas, cinerarias and cyclamen, took their place. Their rise to acclaim seemed to come in tandem with the growing use of cut flowers as table decorations to make the overall effect of a room's décor one of colour and prettiness. Cut flowers, by that time cheap and plentiful, then took over and house plants became unfashionable apart from pots of cyclamen and cineraria when they were in season.

Interestingly, in America, Scandinavia and other parts of Europe, house plants remained fairly constantly in fashion and it was from America and Scandinavia that interest in green plants was now being generated back to Britain. This was furthered by fashionable magazines showing house plants complementing Scandinavian furniture and by films that featured American homes. Another contributory factor to their new popularity was that more people were becoming flat dwellers and, missing their gardens, wanted greenery in their home. Also, house plants fared better in centrally heated rooms than cut flowers.

By the early 1950s florists, particularly metropolitan ones, were beginning to see a return to house plants, especially if they'd taken the trouble to group them into attractive displays rather than have them dotted around the shop. House plants had their advantages. They lasted in the shop and didn't have to be sold within three or four days and they were useful for weekend displays and for putting in the window overnight. As time progressed, house plants were, of course, also to prove a boon to florists who undertook decorating hotels, offices and other places of work.

Twenty years on from receiving the nine pot plants from Constance Spry, Thomas Rochford was given an award by the British Flower Association for the improved development of his growing business and 'making the name "house plant" almost synonymous with his own'.

During the 1950s there was growing interest too in flower arranging, from both professionals and amateurs. It was aided by the arrival, in 1949, of a new florist's sundry which, if the story behind it is true, came from Ealing Film Studios. The tale is that after the filming of *Scott of the Antarctic* (released 1948) there remained great mounds of artificial snow, and this formed the basis of Florapak. The product was a white block which could be cut to fit into vases or baskets. After it was

A Victorian illustration of beautiful-leaved plants.

moistened a little, flowers pushed into it would remain fairly firmly as they had been put in. Prior to this, crushed chicken wire had been the general method for holding flower arrangements in place.

The sundries firm that pioneered Florapak was Cocquerel's of Covent Garden. Albert Cocquerel started selling wrapping paper and minor florists' sundries in Henrietta Street, London, in 1934. When the war ended Albert's son, Dudley, was demobbed and became the driving force behind the business. His brother Cecil joined him to look after the order and stock control side of things. It was Dudley who found Florapak, arranged to have it manufactured and got a special company to market it. It was advertised with hints that it helped flowers last longer, due either to the small percentage of formalin in the block or the fact that water evaporating from the block kept the flowers cool. Much was also made of the ease and speed it afforded. The following quatrain is from a June 1951 advertisement:

> *MISS SLOW'S arrangements all go wrong*
> *You'd think she's lost the knack;*
> *MISS SWIFT'S go smoothly, as a song . . .*
> *She uses Florapak!*

In the florist's shop, Florapak was not without its critics. One florist, looking back, says its minuses were that it could never be used twice, it was difficult to cut without it crumbling and if anything of weight was inserted into it, it broke.

However, in 1952 Florapak was refined and relaunched. Ken Rigeon was a salesman for Cocquerel's at the time, having met Dudley in the forces and started with the firm just after the war. He recalls that Florapak worked well. 'It was the first of a series of cellular foundations, being followed by Bloomfix, Geefoam, several others and ultimately Oasis®.'

Also at that time Interflora arranged for some of its most gifted florists to give floral demonstrations to its members. The venues were cities such as Cambridge, Birmingham and Glasgow but, although it meant travelling miles and arriving home very late, many country members willingly made the effort to attend the demonstrations. An appreciative Sheffield florist recalled: 'One demonstrator was a sheer joy to watch and her absorbing love of her work seemed to steal into you and make you long to be able to do the same.'

However, not all flower demonstrations being given then were so rapturously received by florists. One professional florist and flower shop owner went to a ladies' club where the speaker showed her audience how to make arrangements with flowers from the garden, wild flowers and twigs. She also showed them how to make containers from honey and jam jars by covering them with bark. Her floral arrangements were excellent and the florist came away concerned, fearing that if this sort of thing became popular it would be detrimental to the livelihood of florists.

An exchange of correspondence began in a trade journal as to the dangers presented by such demonstrations, which were becoming a trend. Optimistic florists saw the trend as beneficial – after all, was it not encouraging the public to use flowers and surely the more flower-conscious people became the more they might want to make gifts of flowers bought from flower shops? There were still some doubters, but they might as well have tried to stop a flood tide, for the requests for talks on floral art given to women's organizations and horticultural groups were rapidly joined by requests by bodies of people who had banded together to form 'flower clubs'.

The first of these clubs was set up by Mrs Mary Pope of Dorchester in Dorset in 1949. By 1953 her club had over 1,000 members. In 1955, after many flower clubs had been formed, Mrs Pope sought the advice of the then President of the Royal Horticultural Society about creating an organization for them and in 1959 the National Association of Flower Arrangement Societies was born. Mrs Pope was its first president.

One of the most popular lecturers to flower clubs was Violet Stevenson. In 1952 she wrote a book called *Flower Arrangement Through the Year* and in 1953 the first *Encyclopaedia of Floristry*. A professional florist, Miss Stevenson did her best to quell the unease with which her colleagues in the trade viewed the flower club movement. She assured them that flower clubs did not want to learn the secrets of the craft, that she had never been asked to lecture on bouquet or corsage making (other than to genuine florists or nurserymen florists) and that flower club members would not constitute commercial opposition. However, she pointed out that it was more or less in the balance whether flower club members became friends or foes of florists and that it was in the interest of florists to keep in the lead as floral artists. She even advocated that if there was a flower club in their district,

A demonstration delights professional florists in Cardiff in the early 1950s.

a florist should join to help and advise. It's not known if this advice was taken, but certainly many professional florists willingly entered into the spirit of public interest in flowers and gave demonstrations in their shops in the evenings.

One of these was Tommy Harrow, a noted florist of Aberdeen who had been in business since 1923. Harrow's senior making-up girl in the 1950s was Alice Wood, who remembers the demonstrations: 'They were held at the back of the shop in a place called "Cults". It was a narrowish building but it could hold a lot of people. There was a dais at one end. A lot of members of the public came and out of it the Aberdeen Flower Club was formed.' Alice was too modest to say that as well as Mr Harrow and visiting experts, she, too, gave demonstrations in Cults.

By a curious coincidence, Robin Wayne, who showed me the Festival of Britain emblem, spent part of his apprenticeship in the 1950s at Harrow's. He wrote diaries of his apprenticeship days and these too emerged when he was clearing out his shop in Swansea. Often in the diaries there is reference to 'Cults studio'. He describes not only his task of arranging flowers in a vase which was artistically placed in a picture frame as part of Cults' décor, but attending demonstrations in the evening. For example, an early entry reads, 'Alice started the evening demonstration by doing a small C.S. bowl of massed small flowers.' 'C.S.' referred to Constance Spry whose style Robin would have been familiar with as in the 1950s he had spent six weeks training at the Constance Spry Flower School. His diary of that time is crammed with diagrams and instructions, from the intricacies of wiring violets singly for fan-shaped 'day sprays' to the words of wisdom gained from George Foss's lecture on house plants.

At the end of his training Robin Wayne took his National Diploma examinations through the Society of Floristry. He recalls:

> Part of the exam was oral, which I'm sure doesn't happen today. I can remember having to sit before two or three lady examiners, who wore hats and gloves, and answer their questions. The exams took place in London Polytechnic on the top floor, which had a glass roof. If the weather was warm the place got very hot, which wasn't very practical for floristry exams!

The Society of Floristry was founded in 1951 and resulted from the inspiration of a florist named Anne Lewis, helped, initially, by two florist friends Mollie Jenkins of Bristol and Margaret Ritchie of Dundee. Their idea was to set standards by examinations and enable floristry to be acknowledged as a profession. The forming of the Society was a much-needed move, for interest in floristry had plummeted during the war years, added to which the Royal Horticultural Society had decided to discontinue its professional floristry exam, leaving no qualifying body.

Jean Harrison (née Ogilvie) received her certificate showing that she had gained a diploma through the Society of Floristry in November 1955. Jean, who had loved flowers and entered local floral competitions in her home town of Cork since she was a girl, explains how she came to take the certificate:

> Constance Spry came to Dublin for a week and held classes at the Gresham Hotel. I went and this made me more keen than ever. I tried to get into the Constance Spry Flower School in London; however, it was full so I decided to go to the London School of Florists at Ravenscourt Park in Hammersmith. I knew Father wouldn't approve, but I sent away my fees for ten months' training and started there in September 1954. The principal was Miss Canning, who'd opened the school after the war. My teacher was Joan Dove, who, oddly enough, had come from Ireland.

Training at the School of Floristry London Ltd and taking the Society of Floristry's exam was to lead to Jean setting up her own business. She explains:

I took the Society of Floristry exam after I finished in June. There were boys and girls at the School and there was one fellow called Wilson Stewart who'd worked in Dublin but his father had moved to Cork. We decided we wouldn't work in London but would come back to Cork. There were no florists' shops in Cork at the time. There was only the English market, an undercover market which had stalls, one of which sold fruit and flowers.

We had some cards printed with our names and 'FLORAL ARTISTS, Diplomas School of Floristry (London) Ltd' written underneath, and in November we put on an exhibition of fresh flowers in Cork. There were buttonholes and wedding bouquets; and it was at the time when painting pine branches and cones was just starting and we did those too.

In February we got a tiny shop, just a ground-floor room with a window, but right in the centre of Cork – just off the main street. Parents and friends rallied round to give us custom and people began to see the work we did. We used to mount freesias on very fine wire and put a piece of damp cotton wool down their throats because when they were taken off their stem they were not inclined to last. People would think you were fit to be locked up if you thought of doing that today. We went to endless trouble. We had a visiting card printed with 'Flowers for Occasions' on it and we'd go through the engagement notices in the paper each day and send this card to the bride. There were very few flower shops in Dublin then – I only knew about two – I don't know if they did similar. Anyway, the brides would visit us, coming in with the card in their hand.

We were very careful to keep up a good standard of work and turned work down if we had too much to cope with. We felt if you can't do it properly, don't do it. I remember after we started in February I got bad jaundice and was out of it for six weeks; then that Easter we had fifteen weddings. We worked from early morning till late at night and my sister fed us in the shop. I sometimes think now of all the things that could have gone wrong, for if we hadn't ordered enough flowers there was no one to go and buy them from. We bought stock each day from a wholesaler in Dublin, and it came by train. We were at the mercy of the wholesalers. Sometimes you ordered say, green orchids, and the box came and they weren't in it – just roses and carnations. Also you couldn't depend too much on local nurseries.

Ribbon came from a florists' sundries merchant in London. I used to go over once a year but when floristry got going in the area the sundriesman used to come over.

People in the country used to go into the woods to get moss for us. Delightful if it was from a wood full of holly leaves! Your hands suffered and were also the worse for wear from chicken wire, which we bought by the roll from a hardware shop.

I remember that when pin holders for flowers came in they helped with bigger arrangements. When there was a film festival in Cork at the Savoy hotel we decorated the stage and did pedestals. We used our own vases and pin holders. Say a vase had five or more big gladioli in it, it could be wobbly but the pin holders added weight. We also had lead weights with holes in and we'd put one behind the vase out of sight. We'd then put one end of a piece of string or wire through the hole in the weight and tie the other end to the vase handle. That held the vase firm and stopped it toppling – very make-do and Heath Robinson!

JEAN OGILVIE and WILSON STEWART
FLORAL ARTISTS
DIPLOMAS SCHOOL OF FLORISTRY (LONDON) LTD.
Wreaths, Bouquets, Floral Decorations to order.
ESTIMATES FREE
KENDALSBRAE,
DOUGLAS ROAD,
CORK,
Phone 23417
15 WILTON LAWN,
CORK,
Phone 22211

Jean Ogilvie and fellow students of the School of Floristry. Jean is sitting on the grass on the extreme left. Wilson Stewart is standing fourth from the left in the third row up (behind the tutor).

Not long after we'd opened, a school of ballet started up and it took the City Hall for a big 'do'. We said, 'We'll do the flowers.' We weren't getting paid but our name was put on the programme. We spent all Sunday afternoon going backwards and forwards from the shop to the foyer of the City Hall and just as we finished two huge urns one of the gentlemen of the committee just walked into one of them and it went flying. We were nearly in tears. It was only half an hour to opening – it was the worst calamity possible. He just walked round it and didn't apologize either. We redid it.

There was no Interflora in the south of Ireland then. I think we were to be the first in about 1958 or 1959. We used to send our stuff by rail or bus – trains didn't even run to some places. We'd send as far as County Limerick, that's about sixty miles away to the north; down to Dingle at the end of the Kerry peninsula in the west; and as far east as Waterford. We had enormous boxes made of strong cardboard by a paper manufacturer to our specifications. They were like coffins. Some were long but the wreath ones were big and square. They were returnable, five shillings each.

Home deliveries I did in a Morris Minor van. We didn't have our name on it. At busy times like Christmas or Easter an odd pal would drive it.

After about a year and a half, Wilson Stewart said to me (it was at the time when people with gardens were getting frightfully interested in flower arranging), 'I'll give some lessons – would you mind?' I didn't mind. I was married by then and went home after work so he gave lessons in the shop in the evenings for a year and from that grew the Cork Flower Club and Wilson was their first president. We judged at their exhibitions and very, very gradually word of the clubs spread in different directions and other flower clubs formed. I thought, 'How are they all going to survive!' but they're still going strong. One of the ladies, Mrs Knox [who helped start the Cork Flower Club], went for a course at Constance Spry and opened her own shop. We were going well by then, so it didn't worry us.

Jean continued with the shop until 1964. Meanwhile, Mrs Knox, who had opened her shop in Emmett Place on Valentine's Day in 1959, had built up a reputation for her style of floristry. Buying a shop had been a bold but characteristic move on her part, for at the time she was aged sixty and recently widowed. Despite the misgivings of her daughters (although her sons-in-law were supportive) Mrs Knox made the venture a wonderful success. Her customers liked her funeral sheaves and she made débutantes bouquets and decorated wedding marquees. She even had orders from the Taoiseach (the Irish Prime Minister).

Mrs Knox's granddaughter, Jane Hawkins (who in later years also went to Constance Spry's Flower School), recalls: 'She was very good with colours. She knew exactly what her customers liked and the colours of their sitting rooms as well! She also did floral decorations at events and decorated for local companies and the Metropole Hotel.'

Jane's husband, Brian, supplies a hint of Mrs Knox's characterful persona: 'On odd occasions I used to drive her when she went out with some of her completed orders. I remember we'd be in the middle of main roads full of traffic and she'd suddenly say 'Stop here' and get out to do her delivery!' Jane adds: 'She got contracts through her personality and because she was known in the city but she was much more interested in doing a job well than in what profit she would make from it. She ran the shop until she was seventy years of age.'

❦

CHAPTER FIVE

Where the flowers came from

For generations there was an unchanging pattern in the market flowers that supplied florists' shops – although there were imports from the Scilly and Channel Islands, Holland and France – flowers were, for the most part, only available in the British season of their flowering. For example, in winter it would have been impossible to buy gladioli. However, by the 1970s flowers were being air-freighted from such countries as Colombia, Israel and Zambia – in fact from all around the world, and this made the old 'seasons' rule non-existent. Now flower wholesalers could figuratively follow the sun.

Of course this state of affairs was a knock to British flower growers, particularly as business from new producing areas flourished. Their flowers grew strong in ideal climatic conditions and expenses of heating and labour were low.

John Godsmark, a retired nurseryman of Sussex, recalls that at one time all his glasshouses were given over to carnation growing but when Colombian carnations began to flood in, he had to change to another crop. By adapting, the nursery carried on and is now run by John's son. John believes that, for the most part, British growers are big nowadays and use sophisticated methods of cultivation.

However, small growers, usually the third or fourth generation of the family in the business, still exist but they too have been affected by the growth of imports. The Hardings of Blunham in Bedfordshire are an example. Jill Harding says, 'My husband's grandfather started the business in the late nineteenth century. My husband's father took over then. When he died in 1975, my husband and I carried on, but of course my husband had been working in the business since he was fifteen! Now our son has joined us.' The Hardings produce glasshouse-grown alstroemeria and column stocks and outdoor-grown Sweet William and statice, and they also sell bedding plants; but their principal crop is, and always has been, chrysanthemums. 'Years ago at Christmas you could take five or six hundred blooms to market and they'd sell them.

Now it would be a struggle to sell that amount because of flowers from overseas. Going back beyond the 1970s there was only English stuff in the market and chrysanthemums had no competition, not even roses, during the winter.'

Since that time the Hardings have relinquished growing the traditional 'bloom' type of chrysanthemum and have concentrated on the 'spray' sort. With the 'bloom', side buds are taken out and all the energy goes into the crown bud but, with 'spray' varieties, the crown bud is taken out and this encourages flowers to spray out either side. Of course they still face foreign competition from overseas growers exporting spray chrysanthemums, but Jill believes that British-grown ones have the merit of freshness and thus a customer finds they last longer than imported ones. It's a view shared by London flower wholesaler, John Collingridge: 'English flowers still have 30 or 40 per cent of the market. They can compete on freshness. They come off the plants today and can be in the market the following day.' Melvin Hall, a manager in the Birmingham Wholesale Market, acknowledges that imported flowers have brought quantity to the markets but he also champions British growers: 'During the summer, as far as I am concerned, 75 per cent of our flowers are English.'

That is a fine tribute for a home industry which over the years has supplied florists; and it is of course through the work of British growers that the flower-shop trade has developed. Take, for example, the story of the carnation, a flower at one time much grown in Surrey, Middlesex and West Sussex. In 1953 the Ministry of Agriculture's Horticulture Commissioner H.V. Taylor wrote:

Towards the end of Queen Victoria's reign the introduction of long-stemmed cut flowers, and, in particular, of the Perpetual Carnation (which was first introduced into this country about that time) provided a new means of table decoration, and this started a revolution in floral decoration and led to the creation of the Cut-flower Industry as we know it to-day. It is said that the Carnation was a primary cause of the cut flower taking the place of the potplant as a table decoration. The Carnations were gayer, lighter and more colourful, and so more in keeping with the mood of the people of the gay Edwardian era.

The perpetual-flowering carnation had first been developed by the French but been improved so much in habit and growth by American nurserymen that in the late nineteenth century it was known as the 'American carnation'. It was a more prolific flowerer than any of the kinds being grown by British nurserymen and American growers were puzzled that in Britain its merits were not recognized. For

Women picking wall-flowers for market.

example, in 1880 one American grower wrote the following to a British horticultural paper:

> I have been surprised that some of the enterprising cut-flower growers from the London trade have not introduced a stock of American Carnation for cut flowers … the price in Covent Garden at the end of October was two shillings to three shillings a dozen for carnations but in New York market at the same time it was four shillings per 100 … I am however aware amongst your varieties there are some few fine flowers but if a plant only yields one a week it is of little value in comparison with the room which it occupies.

British growers, however, continued to be reluctant to take to the American carnation. Its 'rough' edge was disliked and also the fact that it tended to split its calyxes. One large British nursery, Hugh Low & Co., did in fact submit a 'perpetual-flowering carnation of the American type' to the Floral Committee of the Royal Horticultural Society and received an Award of Merit for it. However, many people thought that the Committee 'lacked both taste and judgement'.

In 1897 a perpetual-flowering American carnation called 'Mrs Thomas W. Lawson' came on the scene and at the time it was reported that the stock of the variety was sold for $30,000. British growers who heard this thought it was a fairy tale but in 1904 the variety proved its worth. A prime mover in the perpetual carnation's rise to fame in Britain was a grower called Alfred James Batchelor Smith. He had a nursery in Enfield, Middlesex, to which the doors were kept firmly shut and at which guard dogs discouraged unwanted visitors. Like a number of growers at the time, Mr Smith was experimenting with plant breeding and the security was to protect his experiments. In 1904 he crossed 'Mrs Thomas W. Lawson' with an English carnation called 'Winter Cheer'. The result was a scarlet carnation which flowered prolifically like its American parent but had the English carnation's merit of not splitting its calyxes. It was thought to be the first great perpetual-flowering carnation raised this side of the Atlantic and Mr Smith called it 'Britannia'. Its fame became such that thereafter Mr Smith was often referred to as 'Britannia' Smith.

In its early days the perpetual-flowering carnation produced only nine flowers per plant a year. However, by the mid-1950s there were varieties that produced twenty-five flowers per plant and it was being described as a marvellous plant which 'flowers every day in the year over a number of years, and is the only kind of flower the florist has in his shop window every day of the year'.

The rose was similarly to be 'improved' by growers as time went by. In mid-Victorian times the most profitable rose to grow was the Moss-type. Many grew it under orchard trees, which protected it from frost. In July, nearly every corner of the streets of London had a flower vendor selling Moss roses which they surrounded by a little fern or the rose's own leaves and wired as a coat flower. A bunch of eight to ten Moss roses could be bought for 6d. Moss roses, like most roses of the time, had a short stem.

During the winter and spring, glasshouse-raised Tea roses were sold. Many were imported from France but as glasshouses became cheaper to build and their heating methods improved, English growers began to compete with the French imports. The most popular varieties were 'Niphetos' (pure white) and 'Isabella Sprunt' (golden yellow). These two formed large, perfectly shaped flower buds which were more sought after in the flower markets than fully expanded blooms. Bouquet makers paid 3s to 9s a dozen for them at Covent Garden round about 1879. Hybrid Perpetual roses weren't grown in glasshouses to any extent, for they proved too much trouble and too expensive to force into bloom and once cut their blooming season was over, unlike Teas, which kept growing and flowering.

However, it was found that despite having scent, form and colour, the growth on Tea roses was usually on the weak side but if a Hybrid Perpetual was crossed with a Tea the outcome was a rose with not only stronger growth but also a long stem, which was a sought-after attribute. Hybrid Teas thus came to the fore as glasshouse roses and, particularly during the 1920s and 1930s, a multitude suitable for forcing were bred. The Irish nursery McGredy's of Portadown provided a substantial number, one of which, 'Mrs Herbert Stevens', was considered to be the best white of its time. Pink was the most popular colour and 'Lady Sylvia', bred by W. Stevens in 1927, the most popular of pinks. In 1924, Stevens had also bred 'Roselandia', a widely grown yellow rose.

Stevens was a well-known firm of rose growers. Its premises were at Cheshunt in the Lea Valley, where they had gone in 1890. The Lea Valley area, which touches on Middlesex, Essex and Hertfordshire, became one of the largest glasshouse growing areas in Britain. From the 1880s nurserymen (no doubt many driven off their sites nearer London by housing development) set up business there. In 1890 there were 264 acres of glasshouses in the Lea Valley; by 1929, 667 acres; and, in 1950, 1,500 acres. In the early 1930s Mr Stevens's nursery alone comprised thirty-eight acres of glass, of which five were given over to tomatoes and the rest to rose crops. I am lucky enough to be able to quote an eyewitness account of Stevens's nursery at that time, given to me by George Dudfield, a retired nursery owner. George went into gardening as a lad in private service but then moved on to work for a chrysanthemum grower in north Cheshire. Before his death in 1998 he vividly recalled the following, which happened around 1932:

> During my spell at this specialist chrysanthemum nursery my employer arranged a long weekend in Essex and Hertfordshire for himself, his two sons and me to visit several specialist cut-flower glasshouse growers in the Lea Valley. One of these visits was to Stevens, England's largest specialist rose growers. The flowers being grown there under glass were mainly for Covent Garden market for the floristry trade.
>
> It was arranged for me to be taken round the glasshouses with the manager in his little Austin Seven at seven o'clock in the morning. He was to visit the various charge hands and give them personal instructions on which blocks to water. I followed him around with a carpenter's auger, which he screwed into the gravelly soil to check its moisture content. I was surprised to be told that only six cultivars of roses were used in this production unit, these being mainly sports of 'Ophelia' with stems two and a half feet in length. I recall in particular 'Roselandia' and 'Lady Sylvia', the latter variety being the most popular.
>
> Each rose bush, planted directly into the earth, was spaced about two yards apart and each bush's branches were pegged down around the parent.

Blooms were gathered, placed into deep buckets of water and quickly transferred to the main packing shed on manually drawn trucks.

I was overwhelmed when shown the packing shed. The building was about a hundred yards in length with a thatched roof which sloped down to about one yard above ground level, the building's brick side being mainly below ground level. Two concrete ramps ran down to two sliding doors at each end of the building to allow access for the fresh cut flowers at one end and ready-packed wooden trunks of expertly graded long-stemmed blooms to be dispatched on waiting railway vans (horse-drawn) at the other end. The packing benches ran the full length of the building, all fitted with sliding doors to allow for the flower buckets to be placed underneath in the dark where the blooms were left for twenty-four hours to take up water. A large number of lady packers dealt with them efficiently the next day.

In those days the packing of quality cut flowers, particularly roses and carnations, was very carefully done. The bloom was placed on 'spills' across the boxes, about four blooms across, three dozen stems to a box.

I never knew how many people were employed at this establishment but they had their own social club and recreation ground.

I was told by the manager that he had started work on this nursery as a boy with the owner and three other employees. I was also informed that the owner, who had retired to a seaside resort, had become the first nurseryman in England to become a millionaire – some achievement in those days!

Fortunes might have been made in the flower trade during the 1920s but come the financial depression of the 1930s, flower buying was reduced. It was a thin time for flower producers, for in addition to the lack of trade, there was stiff competition from imports which in those days came mainly from France, the Netherlands, the Scilly and Channel Isles. Even though prices were low, importers continued to send stock as Britain was their only outlet. Wholesalers in markets were glad of the many street sellers operating at the time, for they helped to keep the markets clear.

Between 1925 and 1931 the value of imported flowers rose from £410,000 to £1 million. The government was anxious to save the home growing industry but didn't want to cut down on imports to such an extent that, in winter, when English flowers were scarce, there would be insufficient in the shops. They devised an import tax which was low on flowers not normally grown in Britain in winter but high on flowers which came in direct competition. The low rate was 2d per pound and the high 9d per pound. However, there was one category which was rated higher still: this was flowers from spring bulbs. Those imported between 1 December and the last day of February were subject to 1s 3d per pound tax and those imported between 1 March and 30 April, to 1s 0d per pound tax.

This is an interesting indication of the extent to which bulb flowers were then being grown by UK producers.

The Scilly Isles had pioneered selling cut flowers from bulbs as far back as the 1860s. Some of their growers, looking for fresh ground, took their skills to Cornwall. Scotland's industry didn't develop until after the First World War but then it proved its worth, and it still does, for because of its colder climate the outdoor flowers bloom when southern ones are over and so find a ready market. However, by far the largest producer of cut flowers from bulbs in 1938, when the tax finally became implemented, was Lincolnshire. Out of its total flower production, 82 per cent was from bulbs.

The Lincolnshire bulb industry had come about by way of necessity being the mother of invention. During the 1880s the agricultural market was depressed and prices for farm produce low. Many farmers in southern Lincolnshire, where the soil is particularly fertile, decided to switch to market gardening and fruit growing, and some also began bulb growing in a small way. Probably at first the latter was merely snowdrops, for it seems that these flowers flourished better in that part of the world than anywhere else, even Holland!

In addition to farmers, there were Lincolnshire people in other trades who began to add bulb growing to their livelihood. Some entries in the trades directories of the time make odd reading – for example in 1892 one William Moore is described as 'Tailor and Bulb Grower'. A warehouse owner and general dealer named John Thomas White was also to become involved in the bulb business. It is believed that originally this came through his handling bulbs for other people and sending them on to retailers in large towns. He began to plant up a few daffodils for cut flowers for the market on his own account; at first less than an acre. Then, in 1890, he bought seven acres of land, complete with warehouses and greenhouses, and turned that to daffodil production. A few years later his acreage had upped to twenty. Other growers had also turned to daffodil growing but not to the same extent as Mr White, who in later years was credited as being a founding father of the industry.

> At Guernsey, as the steamer hove to on her return, to take in, and discharge, goods and passengers, a large basket of flowers was handed up the ship's side: 'They will be 1s 6d,' said the waterman. I afterwards traced them to the cook's cubby and found they consisted of nine large bouquets, for which the cook obtained sixpence each at Southampton. Flowers were among his weekly prerequisites.
>
> *The Cottage Gardener*, 30 September 1852

Bunching narcissi in the Scilly Isles, in 1893.

Bordering parts of Cambridgeshire shared the same soil properties as south Lincolnshire and around the turn of the century two more growers, Mr R. H. Bath and Mr W. T. Ware, began planting narcissus at Wisbech, Cambridgeshire. Mr Ware's interest in the daffodil as a cut flower for market went back to earlier days. In 1878 his father had seen a new Poeticus narcissus called *Narcissus poeticus ornatus* in Covent Garden market. Mr Ware senior found out that the flowers of it were being grown by Mr Poupart of Twickenham, Surrey, who got the bulbs from bulb merchant Mr Barr of King Street, Covent Garden; he in turn had obtained the bulbs from Paris. The trail then went cold, for sources were carefully protected. In 1882 or 1883 the two Wares, father and son, decided to go to France and find *Narcissus poeticus ornatus* for themselves. They had no idea where to go, but after making a few guarded enquiries in Paris they set off for the outlying regions. How they got on is told in an interesting article written by G. W. Leak for the *Lincolnshire Magazine* of 1932, quoting from a letter written by W. T. Ware:

> With a frugal lunch in our pockets we forthwith began to explore and tramped around for miles, looking into walled gardens and peeping over walls until we found a grower of Poeticus Hatif, as they called it. I was the interpreter: my father a gentleman from London. 'Have you any bulbs of Poeticus Hatif?' I said to a sharp-looking man in blue trousers and blouse. '*Mais oui*,' was the reply, 'but the price depends on the quantity.' '*Mais certainement*,' I said. At last a bargain was struck. Twelve francs a 1,000 for a parcel of 10,000 to 15,000.

The Frenchman also got his neighbours to supply the Wares and a million bulbs were sent to them. It was a satisfactory arrangement and further bulbs changed hands until the Wares had sufficient of their own stock to put *Narcissus poeticus ornatus* on the market.

W. T. Ware also raised and introduced a narcissus called 'Fortune', which was a very popular commercial cut flower.

Tulip growing in Lincolnshire didn't really begin until a type called Darwin was introduced in about 1905. Long-stemmed, vigorous and in a great variety of colours, Darwins obviously had market potential. Mr Ware was the first to plant them, at Wisbech.

Bulb forcing began in the Lincolnshire/Cambridgeshire area around the 1920s when glasshouses began to be erected. By the 1930s there were 150 growers in the Spalding area sending out 100 tons of flowers per day (6,000 tons in a season).

The Lincolnshire industry continues to this day, with most of the flower growing being done in the Spalding and Boston area. The principal crops are daffodils and tulips. Since 1959, Spalding has held an annual flower parade in which beautifully decorated floral floats proceed through the town. This occurs usually on the first Saturday in May.

Today there are two major UK flower crops. One is spring flowers (although spray carnations have tended to take over from tulips) and the other is spray chrysanthemums.

Bloom chrysanthemums used to be widely grown. Terry Headey, who started work on his family's nursery in Dunstable in 1945, recalls how many 'blooms' they produced:

> We used to grow 10,000 in ten-inch clay pots – you could wheelbarrow six pots at a time. Each pot would take three rooted cuttings (the cuttings were taken in January). In the summer the pots would stand out, and then, in September, be wheeled into the greenhouses. There would be three stems on each chrysanthemum so one pot would yield nine blooms. We packed the cut flowers in wooden boxes, three dozen in a box. Before there was much motor transport a horse-drawn trolley would come and be loaded and taken to the station. The boxes were addressed to places like Glasgow market. There used to be a wholesaler there called McCaig and Webb. Looking back I wonder how it can have been profitable to them and us!

Pre-Second World War, when George Dudfield was working at a chrysanthemum nursery in Lancashire, he and his employer's sons not only sent chrysanthemums to Manchester's Smithfield market but every now and again transported themselves there too.

> We went to see other growers' packs coming in from distant parts. One agent had some outstanding packs sent from a large grower in Uxbridge called Lowe and Shawyer. I didn't know at the time how big their nursery was. I'd only heard rumours and I'd also heard how it was practically taboo for other growers to knowingly be allowed to get past their gates! The quality of the blooms and the first-class grading of their flowers left a lasting impression on my mind. The agent usually took the lid off the topmost trunk on his pile to display the flowers. L. & S., as they were popularly known, seldom put the name of the variety on the label at the end of the wooden trunk – usually it was just 'No. 1 Bronze', 'No. 2 Yellow' and so on. They always had the first pick of the seedlings raised by a well-known southern chrysanthemum specialist.

An article on the history of the chrysanthemum written in the 1950s confirms how many fine sorts originated at L. & S. and adds 'most of these were not officially distributed but found their way into commerce by devious methods'. George's memories are illuminating on this point:

> Some of my firm's blooms were delivered direct to florists' shops in the Manchester area. One of these had a kiosk in a local town which did very good business. Besides taking flowers from me he frequently bought blooms in Manchester market, mainly those which had arrived from L. & S. He used most of the flowers for what was a considerable wreath trade and so was left with the stems. These stems found their way via our van driver back to our nursery where they were well and truly inspected for any traces of leaves with signs of a basal shoot in them. We, possibly like other growers, soon possessed stocks of the prized L. & S. sorts but usually by that time they had discarded the varieties and were introducing newer types to the market!

By the mid-twentieth century it was a matter of pride and wonder that improvements to early, mid-season and late varieties had made the chrysanthemum cutting season stretch from July to January. Today, all-the-year-round cutting is the norm.

This has come about through a number of reasons. Scientific researchers discovered that different plants react or do not react to the length of the day. These plants are divided into three categories: 'short-day'; 'long-day' and 'indifferent'. 'Short-day' ones flowered more quickly when the days were short; 'long-day' favour long days and 'indifferent' show no particular reaction to short or long days.

The chrysanthemum is a 'short-day' plant and its flowering time can be quickened by 'blacking-out' a greenhouse or lengthened by applying artificial light on dull days. This applies to all chrysanthemums but it was found that the American spray kind was most adaptable.

'Ask any Florist which cut flower he would choose to have in his shop, if he was limited to only one variety, and it's a blood orange to a hayseed he would reply "American Spray Chrysanthemum,"' a grower wrote in 1961, and it was during the 1960s that spray chrysanthemums began to be grown commercially in quantity. The older 'bloom' type is still grown but not to the extent it once was. Of the American sprays the easiest to grow are Reagans. Jill Harding's family grows them at their Blunham nursery. They plant in beds in their glasshouses and the cycle is 'plant a unit and cut a unit' all the year. Reagans are the spray chrysanthemums you are most likely to see in flower shops for their other virtue is long vase life. Spray chrysanthemums are also easier to pack than the traditional bloom type.

You might be forgiven for thinking that chrysanthemums can be perfected no further, but you'd be wrong. It seems they have to be a certain height before you can switch the light on to them to stop them budding up. Presently it takes twelve or thirteen weeks for them to reach this height. However, work is going on to try and make them grow faster, say in nine weeks or less. Breeding is also being done to find new flower forms, for these are always wanted.

Anticipating the popularity of different colours can be a bit of a lottery. Jill Harding comments:

> We order our chrysanthemum cuttings a year in advance and always grow a lot of yellow and white, then we have reds to pinks to bronzes to purples. We also grow fancy ones which are bi-coloured and even green ones, but there can be trends when everyone wants one particular colour. I remember in the year Fergie [the Duchess of York] got married everyone wanted salmon! Also flower shops buy differently. One chap doesn't want pink and another wants a lot of red and bronze.

The practice of shops getting their flowers direct from the grower is becoming something of a rarity. Most rely on a local wholesaler or 'flying Dutchmen'. The latter are Dutch wholesalers who buy at the Dutch flower markets, travel to Britain and deliver either to order or call at flower shops and sell from the back of the van. Years ago, however, there were any number of small growers who supplied local shops, just as there were in Victorian and Edwardian times, and in some cases shops had their own nurseries and the bigger the floristry business, the bigger the nursery. Up until comparatively recent times William Strike Ltd, for instance, had its own large nursery at Yarm in Yorkshire. This supplied the firm's dozen flower shops. Some of the shops were in the main Yorkshire towns, others in Teeside and one in Birmingham. The nursery was beside a railway station and for years it was very convenient to dispatch flowers by rail. Many were destined for the firm's central floral workrooms at their headquarters in Thornaby-on-Tees in Cleveland.

One of Strikes' many shops which were supplied by their own nurseries.

Although the nursery provided the backbone of flowers (and continued to do so until the last of the firm's shops closed, when it converted to crops for garden centres), the firm also bought flowers. Waynman Strike, the last generation of the family to be a florist, says: 'The shops were grouped into areas under the control of a buyer. Each area was based on a local wholesale market which mainly handled bulk from major growers around the county. Our specialist flowers came by rail from Covent Garden.'

Which leads us to another important source of flowers for florists' shops, for specialist flowers and the everyday sort: wholesale markets. The most famous of these is Covent Garden, London's major wholesale flower market. Today it is called New Covent Garden, for instead of being in the city centre it is at Nine Elms, which is between Clapham Junction and Vauxhall. The move took place in November 1974 but a number of people look back to the old site with nostalgia, believing that the old market had more life and good characters. Also, the flexible, lockable 'stockades', which provide security for each trader's stand in the new market, seemed alien at first. One florist customer remarked just after the move, 'Flowers don't seem right in cages.'

It is hardly surprising that the old site should have engendered such a spirit of loyalty for flower trade people had sold and bought there for generations. It was as far back as 1671 that Charles II granted a charter to the Earl of Bedford to hold a market in Covent Garden Square. The Bedfords had acquired the site in 1552 and their connection with Covent Garden was to last for over three and a half centuries – they finally sold the site around 1913. In 1552, on a grant from the Crown it was described as 'the Covent or Convent Garden', for it had been the site of a garden established by monks from Westminster Abbey. Seven acres of land lying outside the garden and known as 'Long Acre' were also granted.

In 1631 the 4th Earl of Bedford set to work to improve his 'piece of pasture land called Covent Garden' and with the aid of architect Inigo Jones erected a church and laid out a piazza or square, making the area the Belgravia of Charles I's time. On the south side of the square was the garden wall to the Earl's residence, Bedford House. Trees overhung the wall and beneath them every Tuesday, Thursday and Saturday nurserymen and market gardeners had stands from which they sold their produce.

In 1678 the Earl granted a lease to Adam Pigott and Thomas Day and others of 'All that market in the Parish of St Paul's Covent Garden for buying and selling all manner of fruits, flowers, roots and herbs whatsoever and also liberty to build and make cellars and shops all along the outside of the garden wall of Bedford House gardens during the full term of six and twenty years, paying the yearly rent and sum of fourscore pounds.'

The market proved a lucrative enterprise. The Bedfords moved to Bloomsbury Square and their Covent Garden house was demolished, allowing more room for the market. In the early 1700s, when Southampton and Tavistock Streets were built on the site of the former house and its garden, the market moved even further into the square. Residents in the stately houses around the square thought it so offensive that they too moved away.

By 1807 it was being written that, 'The market is a filthy scene, soiled by putrid refuse, leaves of cabbage, shells of peas, and roots, the air of which is impregnated with a stench that is wafted in every direction by the wind; and yet the centre walk

An early engraving from the Illustrated London News *showing workers in the flower market at Covent Garden.*

W. B. Gardner sc.

has many attractions for the botanist and epicure, who may there feast their eyes and their appetite with rare and beautiful flowers and rich fruits – but not at the cheapest rates.'

In 1828 Parliament passed an Act of Improvement on the market and the Duke of Bedford, at a cost of £50,000, built a large building to encompass the shops and stalls in an orderly way. This was used mainly for fruit but a few years later open-air accommodation was gained on the roof at the entrance to the market, facing the back of St Paul's church, for the sale of plants and flowers, which were also sold in the open area opposite St Paul's. It was here that, as we have seen, the first florist growers had their stands and the flower girls bought their flowers. In 1872 a flower market with frontages on Tavistock Street, Wellington Street, Russell Street and the market square was built. An annexe was added to it in 1903.

The whole market complex was notorious for the congestion caused by arriving and departing produce. An article in *The Garden*, 9 October 1880, observed: 'The mere wasted labour, the "friction" of getting the carts and the produce in and out of Covent Garden in the morning, or rather in and out of the crush of carts which choke all its streets as well as the market proper, is enormous.'

Buying conditions within the market were also not to everyone's taste. In the 1930s a West End florist writing in the *Bulletin of the British Flower Marketing Association* (a body of growers, market salesmen and shop owners founded in 1917) commented critically:

> Take first of all the market itself. When I say 'the market itself' I mean the covered-in hall. To me this seems to be a most inadequate background for the reception of goods such as flowers and plants. The impression one gets is as if boxes of flowers and plants had been put up for sale in the middle of Paddington station, expecting there to see the full beauty of them! I am fully aware that, for some purposes, such as for very tall Palms, this might be quite appropriate, but I fail to see how the terrible height and that miserable background can add to the beauty of flowers and so help their sale.

Janet Carter of Joe Austin's, Oxford, remembers buying at Covent Garden market:

> I used to go with Dad twice a week to Covent Garden. We had to be there at 3.00 a.m. because if we arrived any later we couldn't get a parking space. A space was kept for us by a porter and he had to be well tipped for it. If a porter didn't know you he'd deliberately put his trolley into a parking space to stop you parking.

In those days the porters carried the big flower baskets on their heads. We had a porter who was most foul-mouthed but it was his normal language.

We also got flowers from our local growers, people like Jacobs and Ryemans. They grew chrysanthemums, carnations, geraniums and lots of ferns. Also violets used to come up from Devon direct to us and a lady in Scotland grew our snowdrops. We used to sell hundreds and hundreds of primroses, snowdrops and violets. They'd come 500 bunches in a box. We knew if they'd been picked by gypsies because they always used wool to tie the bunches. Bunches of heather came from Cornwall too and if people living locally had an orchard with narcissi growing in it under the trees, they'd bring in bunches to sell to us. There were fresh flowers every day.

Often during the week Dad would buy over the phone from Covent Garden market. A wholesaler, for instance Page's or Multiflora, would ring up and say they had so and so and if Dad agreed to buy so many they'd put them on to the 9.00 a.m. train and we'd pick it up at the railway station.

As the first rain that London has seen for 12 days spattered viciously on the glass roofs at Covent Garden this morning, the faces of the flower salesmen lit up and they began to breathe sighs of relief. They saw in it an end to heavy sendings of tired-looking blooms and florists' diffidence.

Business today was slow, and apart from Cars [carnations], which showed a slight rise, prices stayed at last week's levels. Trade in pot-plants was slow too.

Nurseryman & Seedsman, 25 August 1949

On the subject of buying at Covent Garden, Joan Jefferies of Turner's flower shop at Hammersmith Broadway in London has a precious little notebook. Joan took on the shop in the 1960s and kept the old name of Turner's. The notebook is Aunt Jo Turner's record of what she bought during 1968 on the days she went to Covent Garden. Tuesday was her usual market day but in busy weeks she went on a Thursday or Saturday too. As she bought, Aunt Jo neatly wrote down her purchases on each page of the notebook. For example, in March Aunt Jo was buying violets: one box of forty-eight bunches at a total cost of £1 12s 0d (Joan commented, 'They're not sold any more – they're not economical. They had to be picked, bunched and sold and you couldn't ask much for them.') Among other items on 27 August she bought, '1 x 36 Esther Reed 10d £1 10s 0d (that is, one box containing thirty-six bunches of the white daisy-like flower Esther Reed at 10d a bunch, total cost £1 10s 0d).

Joan Jefferies at her Hammersmith shop in London.

For the most part the entries are straightforward but every so often there is one that is mysterious to the uninitiated in flower-buying. Joan translated these oddities thus:

Aunt Jo	*Joan*
Spikes	Daffodil leaves – hard to find today
Blind Mick	Tight-bud Michaelmas daisies
Wedge	*Iris* 'Wedgewood Blue'
Curly	Greenery for wreaths
Asp	Asparagus fern
Peye (or Pye) (e.g. '1 x 26 Red Pye')	Pyrethrums
Fluffy	Greenery
ABs	Large incurving chrysanthemum blooms 'American Beauty'
Pap	Paper-white narcissus
Roddy	Rhododendron branches
John	John Innes compost
High	Hyacinth
Spring	Asparagus sprengeri fern
Mazie (e.g. 3 mazie 5/3d)	A wire mesh flower holder

Just outside the market there used to be another flower-selling venue, the huge premises of George Monro Ltd, on the corner of Tavistock Street and Wellington Street. 'It was like a department store – even had its own canteen,' remembers John Paynter, who worked for Monro's as a junior salesman.

The Monros started off modestly in Covent Garden market in 1862. From his stand, No. 482 in North Row, George Monro sold produce grown by his father. In about 1892, George, with his three sons Eddie, George and Bert in their teens, and no doubt helping with the business, started a new venture – selling cut flowers on one or two small stands in the market. After about ten years George junior, the second son, made the flower-selling side of the business his domain. By then trade had developed so much that the firm bought 4 Tavistock Street and rebuilt it in 1912. In 1933 George Monro bought 43 King Street, one of the great town houses once owned by aristocracy in the days when Covent Garden was a fashionable promenade, which looked out across the Piazza. The firm had previously bought 40, 41 and 42 King Street. In 1936 it purchased premises facing Wellington Street and Tavistock Street. These premises contained, *inter alia*, a ham and beef shop, a theatrical costumiers and a cigarette shop. All were rebuilt to form 22–28 Tavistock

Street, which had large illuminated letters, 'G.M.', shining from the centre of its exterior and housed Monro's flower department. The department had five sections on ground level and a basement and sub-basement beneath. The basement, ground floor and first floor were given over to flower sales and pot plants were sold on the Wellington Street frontage.

George Monro junior was a stalwart and respected figure. He founded the British Florists' Federation in 1918, was President of the British Carnation Society and in 1934 was awarded the Royal Horticultural Society's highest accolade, the Victoria Medal of Honour. He was also known for his kindness. When the journal *The Gardener's Chronicle* faced huge repair bills on its offices, which it found difficult to meet, he allowed it to move into part of his Tavistock Street premises and the repair estimate was torn up. He also came to the rescue of Interflora during the Second World War when a bomb fell outside its office in Bedford Street by clearing a portion of the sales floor in Tavistock Street for them.

When George Monro junior died in 1951, the flower department continued to prosper, with departments for orchids, 'longies and lilies', spring flowers of all kinds, chrysanthemums, foliage, roses and carnations, gladioli and a Continental department. Each section had its own trained staff who had specialized knowledge of their group of flowers.

Many provincial florists used Monro's, either placing telephone orders to it or visiting in person and not venturing into Covent Garden market.

When the market transferred to Nine Elms in 1974, Monro's went too and for the first time for almost three-quarters of a century moved back into the market. John Paynter remembers that, 'It was an enormous change. They found competition five yards away and buyers coming to them of course began to realize what an enormous choice there was once they were among all the stands.'

ENQUIRY: Could you give me any information respecting the value of flowers? I am in the habit of supplying a small basketful of choice kinds, such as Camellias, Ericas, Acacias, Azaleas, Daphnes, Roses etc. …
REPLY: We do not know the size of the small basket referred to. A friend of ours sends a box frequently to Covent Garden – say 2 feet long, 1 foot wide, and 8 or 10 inches deep – firmly packed with such flowers as those alluded to, and perhaps a few Pinks, and some trusses of Stephanotis; and after defraying carriage &c., the dealers generally allow from 25s to 30s. Of course, a gentleman purchasing would have to pay more than the double of that money; as florists must live, and pay rates and taxes, and find skill and taste for the making of flowers after they obtain them. When I used to be about London, flower dealers used to give to nurserymen and growers about 12s per dozen for Camellia blooms, for rather more than three months of the year. Good roses would bring as much, and so would a truss of Stephanotis bloom, and Heaths and Azaleas in proportion. As the days lengthened, the value of the flowers decreased. Our friend, who sent fine Rose buds, and Cloves, and Pinks, and Carnations and some extras from the stove, in the shape of Passion Flowers &c. in June and July, could not obtain more than half of that allowed in March and April.

Exchange between a reader, Pro Bono Publico, and correspondent, Mr R. Fish, in the *Cottage Gardener & Country Gentleman*, 25 May 1858

About thirty years ago Monro's merged with Fyffes Limited but have since been bought by the Page Group, a business that started very much as Monro's did, with a grower renting a stand in Covent Garden market and selling his own produce. John Paynter became a managing director of Page Monro Ltd – so he came a long way since his junior salesman days, although being a salesman was a revered job. 'Salesmen walked on water, almost, in those days,' he said.

John told me about a well-known figure at Page's, Carlo Naef, who had married the granddaughter of the founder of Page's in the 1920s and became very much a part of the company. Retired florist Jim Segar, when reflecting on who had been respected and influential at Covent Garden, had also mentioned him, saying 'people looked up to him'. John remembers:

Carlo was very much a new boy to flower markets when he married June Page, but he was clever. At that time daffodils came from the grower with the bloom open, two dozen in a box. He told the Spalding Bulb Co., 'Send them all in bud.' When a batch arrived he sold them for half the normal price. Of course people bought them because it was a bargain price but they also found that they kept longer and looked better than those which were sold open. By the second consignment he put the price back up to normal but people still bought and from then on no one would buy daffodils unless they were in bud!

I knew that growers send their flowers to the market and then the salesmen sell them for the best price they can achieve and take a percentage of that sale price, but I wondered how the sale prices in the markets were fixed. There appeared to be no price tags on any flowers. John explained: 'I make a judgement on prices in the morning in the first few moments. A salesman tells you the price if you ask. Obviously, it can vary from customer to customer, depending on how big the order.'

Long hours are the norm for market people. John Paynter says:

Mondays and Thursdays are the busiest days. I come in at 12.45 a.m. on both and the rest of the staff are in by 1.30 a.m. In order to get in so early I go to bed between 2.30 p.m. and 6.00 p.m. Then I get up for a while, then return to bed and am up again at midnight to be in here at quarter-to-one. On Wednesdays it's a 3.00 a.m. start and on Tuesdays and Fridays 4.00 a.m. There was a time years ago when on all days it didn't open until 5.00 a.m. – but it gets more and more difficult as the market opens earlier.

In fact, at one time the market did not open for trading until 6.00 a.m. John Collingridge, 'guv'nr' (managing director) of John Collingridge Ltd, who by 6.30 a.m. – the best time to talk to him – has been attending to business in the flower market and in and out of his office above the flower market for a good many hours, explains:

Not many people lived near the market years ago and it wasn't until you got independent travel that it began to open earlier. My grandfather, who started our firm with a friend in 1890 used to live at Camberwell. He'd take the first tram from there which went to the Strand and could be at the market at 6.00 a.m. opening time.

Horse-drawn vans of produce used to come up to the market in the evening. The horses knew their way to the market. Some carters would go into the pub while the stuff was being unloaded and come out drunk but their horse would get them home safely. Of course it was all horse-drawn in those days. In fact one of my aunts married a carter contractor called John Sullivan whose business dealt with a lot of the market produce. His stables were off Drury Lane and they were two-storey.

Transport apart, I asked John what the main difference would have been in Collingridge's business years ago compared with the present day.

Years ago we used to be looking for supplies desperately; now we have supplies from all over the world. Even when I started in 1962 we used to encourage production, suggesting to growers they grow tulips rather than cauliflowers. Grandfather helped to set up a flower exporting company in the Channel Islands and Father went out there a lot.

Between the wars there was a big French business and even a separate market here for it – flowers like anemones, white narcissus and mimosa came from the south of France. They'd come across by ferry and were taken to the rail depot in London's Hither Green. Of course during the Second World War the flower business virtually stopped. People were so hungry in the Channel Islands that they ate the tulip and daff bulbs.

After the war it was mostly English production; then the French business started again. There was a chap called Harry Miles whose father ran a flower wholesale business in the market. During the war Harry was stationed in France and because he could speak French was in the censoring department, but he must have also made it his business to find out about

Left: The firm of J. Collingridge in today's modern market and (opposite, top), the founder, John Collingridge (right), in the old Covent Garden Flower Market, c. 1912.

Opposite, below: Collingridge's premises at 36 Wellington Street, c. 1910.

the French nurseries for immediately after the war he scooped the French trade! Harry died not long ago, aged ninety-nine.

Melvin Hall of Birmingham Wholesale Market confirmed that the flowers there used to be seasonal ones, too, until about fifteen years ago when they began to be imported from overseas in quantity:

> You get freesias and roses all the year round from the Channel Islands, although in winter months the quantities of roses drop, but there arc also roses from Israel and Kenya from autumn through to spring. Carnations are the same as roses – spray carnations from the Channel Islands June to October then Spanish and Turkish ones, and Colombia has all-year supplies. With spray chrysanthemums there are also English all-the-year-round growers.

The quantity of these flowers and the fact that growers supply the market direct have contributed to Birmingham's reputation as a large flower market in its own

A familiar sight in Birmingham – street flower seller Katherine Kelly outside the Bull Ring. She is carrying on a family tradition as her grandmother, Ellen Kelly, and her mother, also named Ellen, were both street flower vendors.

right. Years ago, like most provincial markets it would have been partly serviced by a supply via rail from Covent Garden.

Birmingham is famous for its markets and for many years, in fact into the 1950s, street flower vendors were in far more plentiful supply than flower shops. The market is in the city centre at the Bull Ring and is unique in that it is the only one in the country to combine the sale of poultry, meat and horticultural produce. Melvin is the manager of Geest's large flower wholesale unit in the market.

The wholesale market opened on its present site about twenty-eight years ago. The old one had been next door. Melvin showed me the site, explaining that it used to have a warehouse for wooden box returns. He also pointed out the spot where the large firm Francis Nicholls had once had premises outside the market (these were in addition to its stand in the market). Melvin said that the market proper had opened at 5.00 a.m. but Nicholls' outside premises opened earlier for the sale of plants and flowers. Buyers, particularly those who had travelled some distance, liked the earlier opening for it enabled them to get their buying done and be back at their shops in good time.

Melvin started his career at Francis Nicholls in 1959, earning 45s a week as a trainee salesman. His work mostly involved 'booking' for a salesman and he worked six days a week. 'There were a lot more "shop" men customers years ago. There's been a decrease in greengrocer/florists. It's not just the supermarkets taking trade but rents and rates are too high and places where some of the shops were have been developed.'

A few weeks prior to meeting Melvin I had talked to a girl selling chrysanthemums beneath a market house in a Midlands town. She had been to Birmingham market that morning to buy them. She said that she was getting used to buying at the market but when she first went she was known as a 'mushroom'. 'What does that mean?' I enquired. 'Someone who's just come up!' Remembering this, I asked Melvin if market staff had their own language. He grinned and replied: 'We still communicate in Klat Kcab Gnals – that's "talk back slang" – and, before decimalization came in, if a salesman tapped his chin it meant "on the chin" or three shillings and a tap on the nose meant "on the nose" or two shillings!'

Christine Hinds, a fourth-generation florist of Bermondsey, London, gave me an interesting example of market slang. Telling me how she, her husband and son all went to buy in Covent Garden, because they could carry the flowers themselves and not wait for a porter, and so they stood a better chance of getting back to the shop early she added, 'Some people think that it's like a supermarket, you can grab a trolley and buy out of the boxes. Not so, although at some wholesalers you can get individual stuff. There are two types of people who go to market, professional and non-professional. Salesmen won't help anybody, they don't like students or amateurs and call them "Connaughts".' At Covent Garden I asked how and why the term 'Connaught' had started and what it meant. No one really knew – until I asked John Collingridge. He replied without hesitation: 'It's rhyming slang – comes from "Connaught Rangers", meaning "strangers".'

❀

CHAPTER SIX

Wedding flowers

'Grannie, mother and daughter – we've done all their wedding flowers.' That's the proud boast of many long-established florists. Their customers' family photo albums attest this fact and show that, like the clothes fashions to which they are linked, wedding flowers have been through many changes – literally rising and falling like hemlines.

Their variability would have shocked Victorians, for in 1870 a slightly rounded bouquet was thought to be, like the parasol it resembled, excellent enough to continue for all time. Although the Victorians likened the ideal shape to a parasol, for the most part Victorian bouquets were round, flat and dumpy. The pattern was row after row of flowers arranged in circles round a centrepiece.

Nineteenth-century convention dictated that it was essential that a bride who had not been married before should wear an all-white dress and her bouquet too had to be of all-white flowers. Myrtle and orange blossom were traditional additions to Victorian wedding bouquets. They symbolized love and purity. The custom of brides wearing orange blossom is thought to have been of Eastern origin. Victorians adopted it with gusto. To them the whiteness of the flower stood for purity, its fragrance was emblematic of excellence and the fact that there could be blossom on an orange tree even when fruit was ripening signified that attractiveness could endure with fruitfulness.

Its popularity led to high prices being asked for it but it was no guarantee of quality. In 1872 one father complained bitterly that, of the expensive orange blossom he had purchased, some had produced a flower that was not orange blossom, and the rest had artificial orange blossom in it. A Covent Garden florist admitted that when orange blossom was dear and scarce some florists used syringa, which was the nearest blossom in resemblance. Also they made imitation orange blossom in hard wax, leather or paper and perfumed it, but he added that this was only when they had 'cheap wedding orders to execute'.

A perfectly white Design, centre Camellia, Azaleas gathered round it, but yet put in lightly, and without trying to force a quite level surface, which is nearly impossible, and here undesirable. Five more Camellias at intervals, mixed again with a few of the largest Azaleas, standing lightly.

A few Orange flowers may be interspersed, and then Lilies of the Valley, or white Heath, or Clematis.

If the former, a few leaves of their own may be used, but they should be of the youngest and the palest kind, belonging to roots which have not yet flowered.

In these snow-white groups a very little green tells quite sufficiently, and no separate foliage need be used at all. The small pale green fronds of Maiden-hair could hardly, however, fail to add some grace and lightness, whatever might be the centre.

Miss Maling, *Flowers and How to Arrange Them*, 1862

A wreath in the hair was deemed to be more appropriate than a bonnet and whether the bride wore wreath or bonnet, a lace veil was necessary to complete her wedding outfit. Whereas the bouquet might have come from a florist, the wreath and veil could have been purchased at a shop selling artificial flowers. Henry Mayhew illustrates this in his *Shops and Companies of London* (1865), in which he describes seeing brides visiting Central Avenue in Covent Garden market to choose their bouquets from the flower shops of Bucks or Mary Johnson, then in Oxford Street observing in the plate-glass window of an artificial flower shop 'a bride's wreath and veil, surrounded by those of the bridesmaids, all ready to be sent home at nightfall' but until that time displayed to 'admiring thousands'.

In 1898 Cheltenham florist James Cypher charged £2 10s 0d for two bridesmaids' shower bouquets and 10s 6d for another bouquet, style unspecified.

By Edwardian times, the introduction of different kinds of flowers and trailing plants, as well as different methods of sending them to market – flowers were sent with long stems where possible – brought about a change of bouquet style. The 'shower' bouquet became popular. This was characterized by long trails – a shower – of fern or, as one florist reminiscing recently put it: 'A bride's bouquet stretched from her bosom to her toes.' The shower bouquet was made on a moss ball. A florist writing in a professional florists' journal twenty-five years ago explained how he remembered these being made before the First World War:

A pad of fine sphagnum moss about the size of a golf ball was made and into this was poked a long hairpin-like 22-gauge wire. Every flower or piece of foliage to be used was then mounted (not wired – there is a difference, you know) on to a suitable wire – 22 or 20 gauge according to the weight of the particular item to be positioned. A slight twist of the ends of the wires eventually made the handle … Bouquets in those days were enormous. At least fifteen inches in diameter at the top with three or more trails of asparagus plumosus reaching almost to the ankles. Hanging down in the trails would be roses or carnations. Stephanotis and Valley [lily of the valley] was sometimes interwoven in these trails. Gutta percha or florists' tape wasn't used in those days. The trails were bound together with 28-gauge binding wire, the more particular florists using green silk-covered wire. At the back was a silver paper frill and the handle was of silver

Previous pages: The Wedding Morning *by John Henry Frederick Bacon, a well-known Victorian painting which shows a bridal bouquet of the time.*

paper. Ribbons were mostly French and wire edged. Some were stiffened with a dressing – very sticky if the hand got hot. Not that that mattered as most 'nace gels' wore gloves.

A simpler style known as a 'sheaf' was also favoured. This was a bunch of elegant flowers cradled on the bride's arm. Madonna or Arum lilies were popular bridal sheaf flowers. However, one high-class florist of the day warned that these kinds of flowers 'connoted a dignity, an austerity even, which is a personal characteristic to begin with, and is (or should be) enhanced by the gown. Brides who have other charms but lack this, should leave Madonna lilies alone.'

Retired Southampton florist, Bob Fowler, recalls that in the 1920s, although some customers asked for Victorian posies, the most popular choice was the large spreading shower type. He says that at that time a bride's bouquet cost 30s, 2 guineas, 50s or 3 guineas. Bridesmaids' were 10s 6d, 21s and 25s.

It was not so much the cost of her wedding flowers as the content of her bouquet, which a Bristol florist brought out to her home, twelve miles from Bristol, for just 4s, that upset Gwen Stock in 1939. It was at a time when florists relied for the most part on getting their flowers from local nurseries.

A bride of the 1920s holding her elegant sheaf of lilies.

The bouquet was a great disappointment to me when it was delivered. My dress was 'redingote' style, buttoned to the waist, a very pale blue in colour and then opening coatwise to show the pale mauve underskirt. I had ordered pale blue delphiniums but, owing to overnight storms, they had to replace these with mauve gladiolus and Sweet Sultan (*Centaurea moschata*) and lots of fern!

In the late 1940s some prospective brides began to appear at their florist's with photographs of small, light bouquets which had no fern in them and requested the same for themselves. A number of traditional florists were horrified at this 'modern style', seeing its origin as the schools of floral art, and decried what they believed to be its artificiality. For example, in order to keep such a bouquet light-weight, natural stems were discarded and all the flowers were wired with wire covered with white tape; and it contained 'pipped' and 'scattered' flowers. Pipping was the wiring of small individual florets from, say, hyacinths or stephanotis. With scattering, or 'feathering', generally done to carnations or chrysanthemums, the florist pulled the natural blooms apart, selected so many petals, graded them by size and wired each one to make up a thin, artificial flower head. The bouquet's slender handle was made of the base of the wire stems wrapped in ribbon. This kind of bouquet was pleasant to carry because it was balanced and did not dip into the bride's skirt. In addition, these rather exquisite bouquets looked good in competitions and photographed well. However, despite their virtues, some florists continued to dislike them and pointed out that even a moderate amount of fern or natural foliage helped set off a bouquet against a white wedding dress.

The 'tape' and the 'green' schools were to argue for years. Be that as it may, wedding bouquets had to reflect fashion and as during the 1950s and 1960s dress-es became more skimpy so too did bouquets. Small sprays resting on a prayer book or bouquets designed like a slender crescent or half crescent were some of the other bouquets that were to usurp the popularity of the shower. However, if a bride had set her heart on a traditional or 'classic' bouquet she could still request one from her florist.

On the subject of greenery, a fashion note in a florists' magazine for the 1949–50 season warned that maidenhair, asparagus or other ferns were out of date and should not be included in a buttonhole. Joan Corles, who at the time was the manager of Birmingham's smart flower shop Margaret Tregoning in Temple Row, believes it may have been then that the fashion arose of curling two or three of the carnation's own spiky leaves behind the bloom.

Alice Wood recalls that when she worked for J.S. Duthie, Florist Fruiterers of Aberdeen, round about 1950, it was not unusual to be asked for a vegetable bou-quet. The request would come from the workmates of a bride-to-be. Alice would oblige by making a bouquet of leeks, cauliflowers, carrots, etc. After work had finished, or on the first half day before her wedding, the bride would be given the bouquet by her pals and with her holding it, they would walk round the works or round the surrounding streets. It was all good-natured fun.

From the 1940s to the 1970s, the month of May was often a quiet time for florists. Bob Fowler, confirms that May was the best time for him and his family to take a holiday from their Southampton shop, partly because the 'bon voyage' trade of the liners was not underway that early in the year and also because it was not a popular month for weddings. 'Marry in May and rue the day' is a superstition which dates back to Roman times. However, May being quiet for weddings was not wholly to do with superstition. The month is near the start of the tax year, which ends 5 April, and from about 1945 any couple earning reasonable wages between them would have tried to marry as late as possible in the tax year because of the tax concessions at that time.

In 1920, following a Royal Commission headed by Lord Colwyn, there was a tax ruling that a single person could earn up to £135 and a married man up to £225 (by way of personal allowance) before being liable to pay tax. Many people then, married or single, did not earn enough to make them liable for taxation. However, in the 1940s wages began to rise and more people became tax payers.

Also, whereas previously those who had to pay tax paid it in a lump sum after the year's end, the year 1945 saw the introduction of PAYE (the deduction of tax from weekly pay packets).

These developments meant that, as the married persons' allowance was available for the whole year, even if the couple married part of the way through the year, on marriage many a husband could claim a tax refund. Consequently many couples had their marriages just before 5 April (the end of the tax year) or even on that date, so that they could claim back the maximum refund. It was a bit like a savings account: you had paid your tax through PAYE each week during the tax year and in that last week could claim back your allowance. A bride of the 1960s recalls their refund was enough to pay for the honeymoon!

Also, a woman who was earning over a certain amount could be two tax people in one tax year. That is, she was entitled to claim not only her single person's allowance but also her wives' earned income allowance, which would be equal to her single person's allowance. Both amounts of course went into her husband's income. For this reason, as October was halfway through the tax year, some engaged couples chose October as their wedding month.

A general revision of tax legislation in 1969–70 changed all this and today's

HINT

TALL SLIM – sheaf or large crescent

TALL FAT – large classic

MEDIUM SLIM – medium crescent

MEDIUM FAT – medium classic

SHORT SLIM – small crescent

SHORT FAT – small classic

A fat person always has a slim bouquet and the size of bouquet is always regulated by the size of the person it is for.

Advice from an employer on relating a bride's shape to the size of bouquet to a seventeen-year-old apprentice, written in the apprentice's notebook in 1957 marriage allowance is so small that there is no incentive to rush to marry by a certain date to claim it.

The two peak wedding times of late March and October brought welcome but frenetic business to florists and preparing wedding flowers – at any time of the year – puts a florist under pressure.

Joan Corles loved her work and was highly skilled at making bouquets (one of her creations was a stunning, delicate bouquet carried by Princess Anne when she opened Central Television studios in Edgbaston), but preparing a wedding bouquet was the task she liked least. 'It took such a long time. Each lily of the valley had to be wound round with fine wire – if you didn't they would go limp; and in very hot weather you had to be careful in case roses opened too much. For the amount of time they took, wedding bouquets weren't very economical.'

This is a view shared by many florists. And having to do the large amount of work necessary for wedding flowers to a deadline could have potentially disastrous consequences, as Prue Headey recalls:

> I was working at Welwyn Garden City Department Store as the florist and we had a big wedding order. At the time I was staying with a friend who worked with me and, so as to get on with the order, we caught a 6.00 a.m. train to work. Unfortunately it was the wrong train – a no-stopping train to London! I was frantic and I hung out of a window and shouted to a porter to phone a message to the shop to start without me. There was only a sixteen-year-old at the shop. I'm afraid that probably when we got there the flowers weren't wired that day – it was all done in such a rush!

Terry Headey, retired nurseryman and florist of Dunstable, recalls that it was a frequent occurrence to work virtually all night if his firm was providing the flowers for three or more weddings the next day. In addition he would have been up very early that morning to buy special wedding flowers, such as lily of the valley, at Covent Garden market.

Fulfilling many orders at once also created delivery problems. On one occasion a florist found that out of eight wedding orders, seven of the customers wanted their orders delivered between 9.00 and 9.30 a.m.; and of those seven, three lived fifteen miles from the shop, in different directions. Despite working until after midnight he was up at the crack of dawn to organize everyone connected with the shop who had access to a car to deliver the orders. When the deliverers returned, practically everyone reported that even though the shop had been told that the requested delivery time was only ten minutes from the time of the wedding, brides were seen in dressing gowns, with their hair in curlers, or dressed in jumpers and slacks. After this the shop made a rule that if wedding flowers were required to be delivered before 9.30 a.m. the customer was told there would be a 5s extra charge. More often than not they hastily decided that delivery could be 10.00 or 10.30 a.m.

The story of florists Prue and Terry Headey's own wedding flowers provides a twist to other delivery tales:

> Terry used to go to Munro's, the wholesalers in Covent Garden, fairly regularly and as a surprise gift they sent three boxes of gorgeous wedding flowers for us, no charge. Trouble was it was a week too *early*. We used them on four other weddings and I made my own bouquet from roses from the garden at home.

Terry Headey looks on as his wife, Prue, demonstrates how she used to wire delicate flowers such as lily of the valley.

Another story of a rushed job comes from Case Bros in Cardiff in the 1950s. The doyen of bridal bouquet making there was Major Eric Roberts, son-in-law of Sydney S. Case. One of Major Roberts's legacies to floristry was to invent the carmen rose. This was economical of material, because it used up old roses which were drooping but still had their petals in perfectly good condition; but it was labour intensive, for it entailed the building up of a large single rose by wiring petals from the old roses, each separately. One can imagine, then, the loving care that went into Major Roberts's work. Case's had a delivery man who had been with the company since the days when deliveries were done by horse and cart and had gone on to drive the delivery van. Unfortunately as time went on it became evident that the man enjoyed a 'tipple'. It is not known whether this contributed to the fact that one morning, while on his way (already a bit late) to deliver a wedding bouquet, he had a slight collision and the bouquet was ruined. He returned to the shop with the bouquet, which, as Mrs Joan Case, writing of the incident some years later, recorded, 'Major Roberts had laboured over for hours.' All was not lost, however, for, as she adds: 'A very experienced senior florist made a completely new bouquet in less than fifteen minutes and it was duly delivered on time!'

Like a number of high-class florists, Case Bros had a special wedding room at its St John's Road premises. On the second floor, it had a big table at which brides

An impressive display in the window of Case Bros, Cardiff.

and their mothers could peruse design books and around the walls were glass-fronted cabinets and racks of ribbon. The wedding room at Harrow's of Chapel Street, Aberdeen, was on their spacious ground floor. Rosanne Hall, who began her training at Harrow's in the 1950s, remembers that the only time making-up staff were allowed down from their upstairs work room to the hallowed precincts of the shop was when they had to talk to a customer in the wedding room.

Today, books of wedding designs that can be pored over on shop counters or in a wedding room are no longer the only source of inspiration for brides. Girls find designs for themselves among the many bridal magazines available. Robin

A 1948 photo of Sydney S. Case inspecting a bouquet. Born in 1869, he was the son of the founder of Case Bros and, until his death in 1955, he was a familiar figure in St John's Square. He was noted for invariably wearing a button-hole of white heather.

Wayne of Swansea, who has been a florist for over forty years, does his best to advise when a customer brings in a design that she has found and set her heart on:

> The photo might be of a bouquet of pink and white flowers and when she says, 'But I'd like my flowers to be yellow and red,' I say, 'If you have those colours it'll look entirely different.' Or she might say, 'I like this bouquet but instead of lilies I'd like roses.' And I explain that changing the flowers will change the whole look. I believe some think, oh, the silly old thing, he just doesn't want to make it.

Nothing could be further from the truth, for he enjoys wedding work.

When Robin makes a bouquet he does not use the modern aids which enable a florist to do away with wiring; instead he prefers to put his trust in his wiring skills. Some florists, though, faced with making a bouquet where there are restraints on time and price, find the simplest method is to use floral foam in a plastic holder. The foam looks like a rounded scoop of ice-cream; the holder is the 'cone'. Flowers are arranged in the foam. There are two sorts of foam: one used dry for artificial flowers and the other used wet. The latter is particularly useful for, say, a bouquet of sweet peas in summer which need moisture to stop them wilting.

Although the heavier (shower) type of bouquet has had a revival, many of today's brides request simple 'hand-tied' bouquets. These are flowers arranged fairly loosely in a 'country-looking' bunch and tied first with twine and then ribbon. Cheryl Hopkins, who now owns Case Bros' shop as well as her family's shop, Treseder's in Cardiff, is frequently asked for hand-tied bouquets. In fact she has developed her own medieval-style ones. These she makes of roses on long stems, with wild ivy wrapped round the stems and falling in trails. Bear grass, sprayed gold and plaited round the ponytail of ivy, criss-crosses and helps to keep the ivy secure. The design is a great hit with brides who are getting married at Castle Coch, whose rounded medieval-looking towers rise picturesquely from the wooded slope overlooking Cardiff. Cheryl's medieval-style bouquets are part of the fashion for themed weddings, inspired by such castles and stately homes, which have become popular since the Wedding Act of 1994 allowed weddings to take place at venues other than a church or a registrar's office (provided that the venue is licensed for the purpose). The theme is carried through all the floral decorations.

The bouquets at royal weddings both reflect the trends of their day and sometimes set them. At the time of Queen Victoria's wedding on 10 February 1840, the floristy trade had barely begun. It is believed that she did not carry a bouquet and she does not mention one in her journals. However, the possibility cannot be totally ruled out, for legend has it that the tall myrtle hedges now growing at Fulham Palace started from a sprig of myrtle from Queen Victoria's wedding bouquet. Jill Kelsey of the Royal Archives at Windsor says that the Queen's mother, the Duchess of Kent, gave her a small posy of orange blossom, which it is thought she wore as a corsage. Her dress was also trimmed with orange blossom and she had a wreath of it on her head.

During the wedding ceremony huge numbers of tiny bouquets were distributed as 'favours', but these were made not of fresh flowers but of wax. Their

At her wedding to Prince Philip, Princess Elizabeth carried a bouquet made by Longman's. After its delivery, and at the eleventh hour, a piece of myrtle from Osborne House, Queen Victoria's Isle of Wight home, was added to the back of the arrangement. The fashion for myrtle in royal wedding bouquets was started by Queen Victoria.

maker, Mrs Peachey, was 'Artiste in Wax Flowers to Her Majesty'. Each bouquet was a white rose surrounded by orange blossom and myrtle and tied with scented white satin ribbon. These waxen favours, if looked after, endured for many years after the event.

When Queen Victoria's eldest daughter, seventeen-year-old Princess Victoria (the Princess Royal), married Prince Frederick William of Prussia on 25 January 1858, she was one of the first brides ever to be photographed. On the wedding morning a daguerreotype was taken – by an early photographic process – of her and other members of the Royal family. The Queen is reported to have said that she trembled and, consequently, her own likeness was very indistinct. Princess Victoria, however, sat calmly and thus the garlands and bunches of flowers on her dress and hair were recorded for posterity. It is uncertain what the flowers were

Opposite: Seventeen-year-old Princess Victoria, one of the first brides to be photographed.

but, for the most part, the decoration was probably orange blossom. Her wedding bouquet, not shown in the photo, was supplied by James Veitch of the Royal Exotic Nursery in Chelsea. The nursery was one of London's most respected horticultural concerns. James's grandfather, John, a Scot born at Jedburgh in 1752, started the Veitch nursery business in the late eighteenth century. At that time its premises were near Killerton in Devon. They moved to Exeter in 1832. Five years later John handed over the business to his son James, who was later joined by his son, also named James. In 1853 the firm bought the Chelsea Nursery and James junior came to London to run it.

There is no record as to what was in the Princess Royal's bouquet, apart from myrtle, but, given the high calibre of Veitch's nursery (one of its specialities was orchids), no doubt the flowers were choice. However, there were rumblings in the horticultural press that it was a disgrace that some artificial flowers had to be used for the royal wedding. Perhaps these were in the bouquets of cornflower and marguerites worn in the hair of two of the bridesmaids. These two flowers would not have been in bloom naturally at that time of the year.

James Veitch's nursery also made the bride's bouquet for the wedding of Albert Edward, Prince of Wales, and Princess Alexandra of Denmark on 10 March, 1863. The bouquet was enclosed in Honiton lace and composed of rare orchid flowers, buds of white roses, and sprigs of myrtle and orange blossom. The myrtle sprigs had been sent by Queen Victoria's special directions from Osborne, the royal home on the Isle of Wight. This probably began the custom, which continues to this day, that royal brides carry a sprig of Osborne myrtle. The Osborne myrtle was a tree which had been raised from a sprig from the Princess Royal's wedding bouquet. The Queen made it known that she wished similar trees to be raised at Osborne from the myrtle sprigs from the marriage bouquets of each member of the royal family.

James Veitch personally delivered Princess Alexandra's bouquet to Windsor Castle on the day before the wedding and Queen Victoria directed that he be given a ticket of admittance to the royal chapel to watch the ceremony. It must have been a proud moment for him. Sadly, a few months later, James's father had a heart attack on the day of his mother's funeral and died in his arms. Robert, James's younger brother, took over the Exeter side of the business.

One of the prettiest royal weddings was that of the Duke of York to Victoria Mary, the daughter of the Duke and Duchess of Teck, on 6 July 1893. The Princess, popularly known as Princess May, had been a friend of the Prince and Princess of Wales's two sons, Albert (born 1864, later the Duke of Clarence) and George (born 1865, later the Duke of York) all her life. She had in fact been engaged to Albert

This charming photograph conveys how flowers played a major part in royal weddings of the time. Prince George, Duke of York, and Victoria Mary had ten bridesmaids who carried large bouquets and also wore corsages pinned to their gowns. The bride's bouquet was chiefly made up of Provence roses.

but in November 1891 their wedding preparations were checked when Prince George was taken ill. By Christmas he was out of danger and recovering. However, in January the twenty-eight-year-old Duke of Clarence fell victim to an influenza epidemic which was sweeping London, and died on 14 January 1892. That spring Prince George and Princess May became engaged.

At their wedding there were ten bridesmaids, who each carried generous bouquets and wore corsages. The Princess's own bouquet of completely white flowers was composed chiefly of choice Provence roses. It had been made by florists Wills & Segar, of the Royal Exotic Nursery, Onslow Crescent, in South Kensington.

When Lady Elizabeth Bowes-Lyon (now the Queen Mother) married the Duke of York in April 1923, her wedding bouquet was a gift from the Worshipful Company of Gardeners. This august body became a Company of the City of London in 1605. Its aim at that time was to improve standards and stop frauds such as the selling of dead seeds or trees. The Company was governed by a master, two wardens and a court of assistants. In a later ruling concerning the Company, no one was allowed to practise 'the art or mysterie of gardening' within the City of London or its surrounding six miles without the Company's licence or consent. There were also restrictions on trading hours and venues for anyone selling garden stuff who had not served the Company's seven-year apprenticeship. The Company ceased functioning in the eighteenth century but was revived in the 1890s. In 1911 it presented Queen Mary with her coronation bouquet. The bouquet was made by a freeman of the Company, Edward Piper, of florists J. Piper & Sons of Bishop's Road, Bayswater, London. When the Company's request to supply Lady Elizabeth Bowes-Lyon's wedding bouquet was granted, that too was made by Piper's. The bouquet was of white roses and white heather – the roses signifying York, the heather Scotland.

In 1947 the Worshipful Company of Gardeners asked one of its florists, Martin Longman, to make the bridal bouquet for Princess Elizabeth (the present Queen) when she married Lieutenant Philip Mountbatten on 20 November 1947. Martin Longman was a second-generation florist, whose father, Martin Lengemann, had been born in the German village of Wolvershausen in 1870, the second eldest son of a small farmer. Martin's elder brother, Adam, decided to go to England, as he felt there were better prospects there for him and when Martin was sixteen he decided to follow Adam, having first been to court to get permission to leave Germany. Martin arrived at Liverpool Street station in London not knowing a word of English. Adam collected him, took him to lodgings and found him a job in a men's hairdressing salon in Mark Lane.

Above: Martin Longman whose firm made the wedding bouquet for Elizabeth II. On the right of the photograph is Connie Fears, the designer of the bouquet.

Left: Connie Fears' original watercolour design for Princess Elizabeth's wedding bouquet.

In front of the salon there was a small florist's shop. After a while the woman who owned it decided she wanted to give it up and Martin took it over. He knew nothing about floristry but took on a German who did and learnt by watching him and going to Covent Garden for stock. The business grew and became successful. In 1895 he married Alice Hulbert, whom he had met through attending a Methodist church at Forest Gate. In 1907 he changed his name to Longman, a direct English translation of Lengemann. He also became a British citizen. The Longmans had nine children (seven daughters and two sons). In addition to the shop in Mark Lane they opened one in Southend.

When the oldest daughter, Alice, was sixteen, she went to help in the shops. Business continued to prosper until 1914 and the First World War. Alice, in a family history written many years later, describes the effect of the war:

> In the first place Father's business suffered terribly – [first because it was] a luxury trade in a way, and then, in spite of Father being a British citizen, it was remembered by some that he had been born in Germany, and in the sudden rush of patriotism which reigned in the country, Germans were very badly treated and in many cases, their businesses were ruined and homes badly damaged. Fortunately this did not happen to us, although the business suffered a lot, and Mother had to dismiss the maids and had very little to live on – we lived from day to day, and she had to work very hard.
>
> Then one day in the Southend shop, we had a number of orders in and Father stayed down [from London] to help us and unfortunately was seen in the shop by a costermonger who had a small flower shop in the lower part of the High Street, and he started shouting, 'There is a German, bloody German' and caused such a commotion we thought he was going to break the windows. I hurried Father out by the back way and fortunately there was a train just waiting to go up to Westcliff, and Father managed to board it and then went home, and I stayed on with Connie Fears [an employee]. A policeman came along and restored order but it was a very disturbing occasion which I have never forgotten.

The family moved out of London until the end of the war. Meanwhile gradually the business built back up again.

Eventually Alice and her sister married, and their brothers, Martin and Tom, returning from the Second World War, carried on the floristry business with their father. Martin joined the Worshipful Company of Gardeners. Thus it was that Longman's came to make Princess Elizabeth's wedding bouquet.

Connie Fears sketched and watercoloured six different bouquet designs, which were taken to Buckingham Palace so that Princess Elizabeth could select the one she liked best. She chose a design that was all orchids. Connie was to make-up the bouquet under Martin's supervision. Martin's son, David, takes up the story:

Orchids were collected from leading growers, both professional and amateur – in fact some of the blooms came from Bodnant Garden in north Wales, the home of Lord Aberconway.

When the bouquet was finished (my father had worked on into the small hours of the morning, putting in the final touches), we had a photographer come to take photographs both of it and some general ones. My grandfather, who still liked to come to the shop occasionally, came in that day and was photographed with Connie Fears and other staff.

On the morning of the royal wedding my father drove to Buckingham Palace with a police escort to deliver the bouquet. When there he was requested to put into the bouquet a sprig of myrtle which had been sent from Osborne House. He put it in at the back.

After the wedding ceremony everyone went back to the Palace for the wedding breakfast and of course the bouquet went too. Rumour has it that at some point a page put it into a fridge to keep cool. I don't know whether that's true but when the time came for everyone to assemble for the official wedding photographs, the bouquet couldn't be found! When the royal couple came back from their honeymoon at Broadlands, my father had to deliver another bouquet identical to the original and wedding clothes were redonned and the photographs taken. Oddly enough the photographs we had taken at the shop of that first bouquet didn't come out! I think that through sheer nerves the photographer made some technical error.

In 1953 Connie Fears and Longman's made the Queen's coronation bouquet, again a gift from the Worshipful Company of Gardeners. After the coronation festivities the Company bestowed on Connie 'the gift of the Freedom by presentation without fine' – a rare honour.

David Longman followed his father's footsteps in becoming Master of the Worshipful Company of Gardeners and went on to make many royal bouquets, including those of Princess Margaret (nothing heavily scented in this, by special request, as her husband-to-be, Anthony Armstrong Jones, suffered from hayfever); the Duchess of Kent; Princess Alexandra; Lady Diana Spencer and Sarah Ferguson.

Right: Princess Margaret's bouquet, made by Longman's for her wedding in 1960.

Opposite: Weddings provide the most creative and enjoyable opportunities for florists. Their bride's and brides-maid's bouquets reflect changes in fashion and the bridegroom and male guests often require more than the traditional, single carnation.

Perhaps because of the incident with the Queen's bouquet, the royal request is always for two bouquets. In fact, David recalls that for Lady Diana's wedding he made three: a prototype in silk flowers for the dress designers and two with real flowers – one for the service and one for the photographs. Each of the latter took five girls four hours to make.

For that wedding, David went to see the bride, and dress designers David and Elizabeth Emmanuel had been present too, so he had some idea of what the wedding dress would look like, although he did not see the finished version. Lady Diana requested a large bouquet, undoubtedly to complement her voluminous wedding dress – and David believes her flowers revived the fashion for large wedding bouquets.

The bouquet measured forty-two inches in length and was fifteen inches wide. In its centre was a cluster of gardenia flowers supported by golden Earl Mountbatten roses. Cascading from the centre were *Odontoglossum* orchids and the shower, falling in three main drops, was pips of stephanotis supported by miniature ivy and tradescantia leaves. As with all royal bouquets it also included Osborne myrtle.

Longman's head florist Mrs Doris Wellham led the make-up team. As a junior she had been present when Connie Fears made the Queen's bouquet in 1947. Also, like Connie, she was honoured by the Worshipful Company of Gardeners.

The designs of both the dress and the bouquet had to be kept secret. Clare, David's wife, recalls that they did not dare delegate the collection of the bouquet flowers and so she and David drove down to McBean's nursery in Sussex to collect fifty orchid plants. The flowers had been left on the plants so that they would be as fresh as possible for the bouquet making. On the return journey they were just about to pull in for lunch when they realized that they would have to think carefully where they stopped, for a carload of stunning orchids was an unusual sight and with the wedding day so close, someone might guess to what use they were going to be put. After the wedding, Clare returned the now flowerless plants. Unlike the subterfuge of the plants' collection, their return to the nursery's vehicle took place in a 'Happy Eater' car park!

David Longman has now retired and has a vineyard in Worcestershire, but one of his daughters, Lottie, carries on in the floristry business.

As important, of course, as the bride's bouquet is the decoration of the place in which the wedding ceremony is to be held. Catalogues of Victorian and Edwardian decorating florists illustrate wonderfully that high society of the day made their nuptial vows amid a forest of hired potted palms, lilies, agapanthus and ferns. Given that pots appear to be liberally dotted on the pew tops one wonders how much of the actual marriage service the congregation managed to see!

Wills & Segar's 1890 catalogue has four splendid illustrations of their wedding decorations in St Margaret's, Westminster, prefaced by the following notice:

Opposite: A typical account sent out from Cypher's of Cheltenham which includes charges for decoration of church interior as well as for the personal flowers.

Opposite, inset: An illustration from the Wills and Segar catalogue of 1890 showing the popular 'graceful palms and foliage plants' that were usually a feature of weddings at that time.

CHURCH DECORATIONS FOR WEDDINGS

We devote special attention to this particular branch of our business, always having on hand a large stock of graceful Palms and Foliage Plants of all sizes specially grown for this purpose up to twenty feet high.

As the style of Wedding Decorations in Churches is influenced to a large extent by the Arrangement, Architecture, and Size of the Buildings, the cost must of a necessity vary considerably. We shall be pleased at any time to meet our patrons at the Church, to receive their commands, make suggestions, and furnish estimates.

The price of a Wedding Decoration may range from Five to Fifty Guineas.

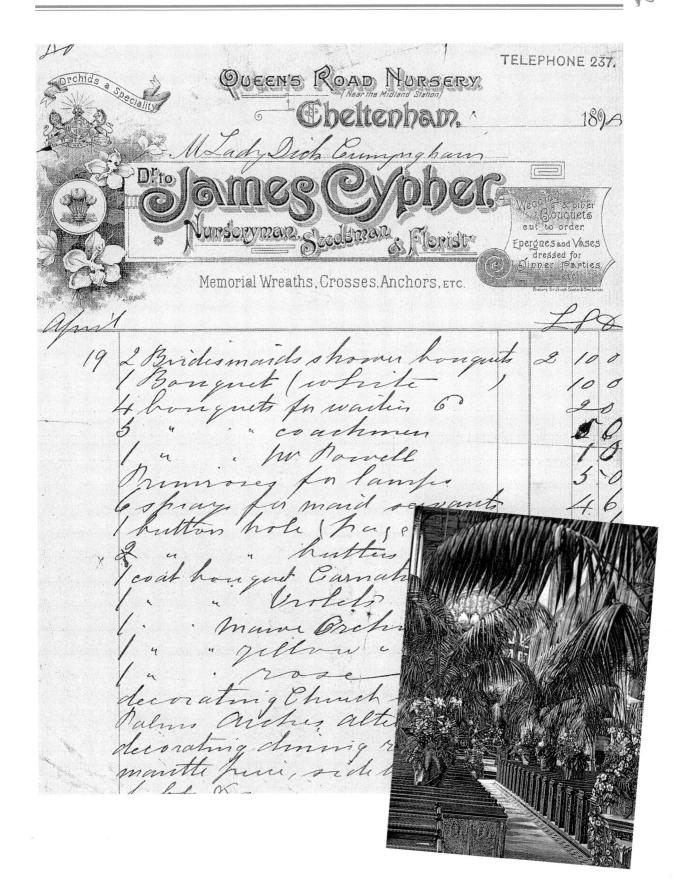

QUEEN'S ROAD NURSERY
(Near the Midland Station)

TELEPHONE 237.

Cheltenham, 189

Orchids a Speciality

M Lady Dick Cunyngham

Dr to James Cypher,
Nurseryman, Seedsman & Florist.

Memorial Wreaths, Crosses, Anchors, ETC.

Wedding & other Bouquets cut to order.
Epergnes and Vases dressed for Dinner Parties etc.

April

			£	s	d
19	2 Bridesmaids shower bouquets		2	10	0
	1 Bouquet (white	)		10	0
	4 bouquets for waiters 6			9	0
	5 " " coachmen				8
	1 " " Mr Powell				8
	Primroses for lamps			5	0
	6 spray for maid servants			4	6
	1 button hole (Mrs				
	2 " " button				
	1 coat bouquet Carnation				
	1 " " Violets				
	1 " Mauve Orchid				
	1 " " yellow				
	1 " " rose				
	decorating Church				
	Palms Arches, altar				
	decorating dining r				
	mantle piece, side b				

Jim Segar, grandson of the firm's co-founder, recalls that this style of decoration, continued right up until the 1940s:

> After the war our work was mainly decorating. The West End of London was our market and for weddings we put groups of plants in the chancel or near the altar. I can remember going back on Saturdays, later in the day to check that all the stuff had come back from the church. Then that style of decoration faded and cut flowers took over, pedestals of them.

Sheila Macqueen remembers how, when she was working with Constance Spry in the 1930s and 1940s, cut flowers took over from pots of agapanthus and ferns as decoration for weddings in churches. 'I believe we were the first to decorate with cut flowers, certainly in the church in North Audley Street and probably in Westminster. We usually did the decorating in the church but we weren't allowed to do that for North Audley Street so we had to get the completed pedestal up the outside steps.'

I asked Sheila if she had gone with Constance Spry to France to decorate the Château de Condé in preparation for the marriage of Mrs Simpson and the Duke of Windsor.

> No, Mrs Spry took Miss Pirie because she spoke fluent French. Although back at the shop we had helped by sending some of the flowers over and, do you know, despite all the hubbub, with all the press of the world at the château gates for the wedding, the Duke of Windsor sent a butler to cut us some wedding cake. When it arrived I slept with my piece under my pillow and then ate it. Miss Derby, who did a lot of buying and was responsible for seeing that all the flowers were in water and conditioned in the basement, kept her piece. When Lord Bath started up his Simpson and Edward Museum at Longleat she offered it to him. By then it was just a few crumbs. He said, 'Can you authenticate it?' She couldn't but he took it and it's probably still at Longleat!

However, Sheila did help arrange the flowers for the wedding of the present Queen in 1947. One of her tasks was helping to decorate two large stone Warwick vases set on either side of the high altar in Westminster Abbey.

Sheila also recalls that for Jewish weddings, of which Constance Spry's team did many in London's St John's Wood and Hampstead, the flower orders were usually lavish. The marriage ceremony takes place beneath a canopy (or chupsa) eight feet square on four supporting poles, eight feet high. Representing the bride-groom's chamber, this is the main object for flower decoration. Additional flowers can be put at pew ends and arranged on pedestals. Often the bride's mother requests that after the ceremony is over the florist takes the pedestals or other movable floral arrangements from the synagogue to the reception. Waiting for all the guests to leave before removing the flowers and then getting them to the reception and installed without causing any disturbance can sometimes prove a taxing matter.

A similar time problem faces florists who have been asked to decorate the same church for a couple of weddings, one following on from the other. Patrick Segar explains:

> If a wedding overruns and your next customer is waiting it's a bit difficult because obviously you can only change the flowers when the first wedding has finished and it doesn't look good rushing round putting in the flowers for the next while they are there!

Prue Headey has occasion to remember the phrase 'Once bitten twice shy' when thinking of a particular order for wedding reception flowers she and her husband prepared at their Dunstable shop:

> Our customers insisted on collecting on Friday all the table flowers and buttonholes and they took them to the scout hut where the reception would be. They put the buffet out too. Next morning they found that the food had all been attacked by ants and came straight down to the shop saying that we'd sent flowers full of ants and they weren't going to pay! Of course we hadn't and it turned out there was an ant problem at the hut. Up until then we hadn't sent bills out until after the honeymoon but then we had to insist on having money on delivery.

Derek Goodyear kindly loaned me some photographs of floral decoration his firm carried out for a memorable wedding reception. His father Edward had been involved in decorating the bride's home for over forty years – 'Goodyear really *were* the court florist's', Sheila Macqueen says. The home was Buckingham Palace and the bride was Princess Elizabeth.

Work for Goodyears began on the Monday before the Thursday ceremony when they were at the Palace to receive, unpack and prepare a large consignment of carnations, orange blossom and tuberoses, which had been flown from the south of France as a gift to Princess Elizabeth. Tuesday was taken up with decorating the state apartments. The following is Edward Goodyear's own description of the task:

> The long buffets in the Ballroom were decorated with handsome arrangements of Chrysanthemums. The colour scheme in the Ballroom was gold and yellow and in the Ball Supper-room all shades of pink. The height of some of the tallest decorations of the buffets was eight feet six inches from the floor. White carnations were used to decorate the entire length of the Picture Gallery, being arranged in the priceless Sèvres vases and bowls. In the Music Room we arranged huge bowls of Mimosa which had also been flown from France as a gift to the Princess.

Wednesday's jobs included dealing with more gifts of flowers, including over 1,000 specimen bloom carnations from the British Carnation Society.

On Thursday, the wedding day, Goodyear's decorated fifteen round tables in the Ball Supper-room where the wedding breakfast was to take place. The floral scheme was white heather and pink carnations, and in among these flowers on the central tables, sprigs of myrtle. These were taken from the plant reputedly raised from some of the myrtle in Queen Victoria's wedding bouquet. This thoughtful addition Mr Edward Goodyear had brought from his own collection of royal myrtle growing at his home in Reigate. His son Derek recalls: 'There were about half a dozen bushes in the kitchen garden. The house was sold after my father died and I expect the myrtles have long since gone.'

Another of Goodyear's tasks before the wedding was the floral decoration of some of the fourteen wedding cakes. To stop the icing cracking under the weight of the flower container plus flowers, the cakes had a pillar in the centre of the top tier. The principal cake, which stood nine feet high and was seven feet round the base, had been made by McVitie & Price, and was being decorated by florists from Constance Spry's shop. They put a fountain of white roses, white camellias and white carnations on the top and around the base a thick ruche of the same flowers. Sheila Macqueen was part of the team. 'I remember a huge garland of white roses round it – it was the cake of cakes.'

It is difficult to pinpoint the date when decorating wedding cakes with natural flowers first began. We know that the practice had begun by 1840, when Queen Victoria was married, for a description of one of her two principal wedding cakes (she also had almost a hundred smaller ones) says that on its top there 'were many bouquets of white flowers. Tied with true lovers' knots of white satin ribbon.'

Opposite: Some of Elizabeth's wedding cakes, fourteen in all, which were decorated by Goodyears. The flowers on and around the principal cake were arranged by florists from Constance Spry.

Archive photographs show, as time went on, cakes became very floriferous. Indeed, when Princess Louise of Wales married Alexander Duke of Fife in July 1889 their seven-feet high principal cake, made by Messrs Gunter of Berkeley Square, London, had, (according to an article in the *Strand* magazine) 'twenty pounds' worth of fresh natural flowers' covering its entire structure.

Gunter's were renowned as royal cake makers but they shared this palm with Messrs R. Bolland & Sons, 'Confectioners and Wedding Cake Makers' of Eastgate Row, Chester. Bolland's were particularly known for sending out their cakes specially prepared for natural flowers: they sank narrow white porcelain cups among the cake decoration so that the stems of each natural bouquet could rest in water. With these devices no reception would be spoilt by the grievous sight of a faded cake.

An illustration from a 1920s Interflora magazine.

CHAPTER SEVEN

Flowers afloat

A year after her 1907 launch, the Cunard liner *Mauritania* gained the Blue Riband award for having made the fastest crossing (it was under five days) of the Atlantic by any liner to date. She held this record for twenty-one years. In the early 1930s, the 762-feet-long vessel was enjoying a less racy but more decorous claim to fame: because of the tasteful wealth of flowers and greenery resplendent in all her public rooms, she was being called, particularly in America, the 'flower ship'.

The Mauritania, *the liner known as the 'flower ship' because of the attention given to its floral decoration.*

The decorative display of plants on board would have been supplied and probably also set in place by a Southampton florist. It is quite likely that a firm of nurserymen florists called F.G. Bealing & Son of Southampton, who had been doing this sort of work for Cunard since 1919, played a large part in the *Mauritania*'s floral fame. Like a number of the very big liners at that time, the *Mauritania* had a gardener on board, whose job was to water and tend plants during journeys.

Bealing's ship decorating goes back to before 1919. Raymond Bealing, born in 1920, the grandson of Francis George Bealing who founded the business in Southampton (his father was also called Francis George), outlines Bealing's history:

Grandfather started in Sholing in about 1889. After a few years he developed a trade with Union Castle Line, whose liners sailed to Cape Town in South Africa. They sailed at four o'clock on a Thursday every week.

A lot of the trade was in little plants in about three-inch diameter clay pots. Plants went every week, mostly little ferns, all grown from spores, using charcoal and sat on a warm pipe in the glasshouse. The pots were placed in mock silver holders put on dinner tables. The Cape Town trip was six weeks, so flowers wouldn't have lasted because six weeks is a long time for cut flowers.

We even decorated the troop ships in the Boer War and at the turn of the century we were providing the liners with corsages for the ladies and buttonholes for the gentlemen to be placed by their dinner plates for the first night on board. These all had to be made up from flowers like carnations and roses. At various places on board there were large zinc-lined containers in which plants and major flower displays were located. These were filled each sailing day.

Ours was still a small nursery at that time, not more than an acre. Then in 1906 we moved to Burgess Street in Bassett (it's now called Burgess Road). There was nothing there really but we'd brought some glasshouses and erected them. We started to build up trade with the White Star Line, who had begun to operate from the Southampton docks. We got a contract from them to decorate the *Titanic* and her sister ship the *Olympic*. When the *Titanic* went down in April 1912, Grandfather lost a good customer! Decorations were plants *and* flowers because the Atlantic run was only five or six days. On the strength of business from White Star, the nursery gradually developed. In the very early days when glasshouse heating wasn't as good as it is today, we had to force half a ton of bulbs to keep up a supply

of flowers. We'd force daffs, tulips, hyacinths, etc., and lily of the valley was very popular at the turn of the century. Our transport in those days was a donkey and cart, which became a well-known sight going down to the docks. Eventually we had twenty-five glasshouses and, when business was at its peak, in fact even before the Second World War, twenty-four staff, male and female.

In Southampton archives there are our old account books and plans showing original workings for what went into containers on board. You could visualize roughly what you needed, subject to season. On one liner, the *Majestic*, there were huge displays of plants near one of the main entrances and in the Garden Lounge two big ornamental barrels about seven feet high.

During the Second World War there was no cruising. But afterwards the *Queen Elizabeth* got going quite quickly after a refit. Then the *Queen Mary* was refitted. They'd both been used as troop ships.

You needed a huge amount of material for decorating and by that time we'd got a two-ton Ford van which just about took all the stuff that had to

The staff of Bealings, Southampton loading a lorry with plants destined to decorate one of the great liners in 1935.

go down to the docks. It was mostly pots, not flowers – that was another load. We took flowers in the hundreds of dozens. It was a lot of work getting it all in order. We'd be up at the crack of dawn cutting inside and out – mostly chrysanths outside. We loaded in reverse order, so that what we wanted first came off first.

We did one ship a week and in busy times in late summer, when American tourists were going back home, three a week.

We had a sailing list and if the sailing time was in the morning we'd decorate the afternoon before with plants and on the morning with flowers.

However, sailing times depended on the tides – big liners like the *Mary* and the *Lizzie* could only sail at high tide or an hour before because at other times there wasn't enough water. If one of them was sailing on the 5.00 a.m. tide we'd put the flowers on the evening before. There'd be a hundred dozen flowers in a mixture of varieties.

There was a lot of preparation before we began work – for example, putting tarpaulin down to protect the floors and carpets, because some carpets were so luxurious you sank in them up to your ankles. We carried the plants on board on handbarrows – like carrying a stretcher.

We'd decorate the passengers' accommodation, the dining tables, the restaurant and the Ballroom. On the *Queen Elizabeth*, there were two large wall vases in the Ballroom which had to be decorated with large flowers like gladioli. Two in the Verandah Grill were difficult to decorate because they were high on the wall and you had to stand on tiptoe to fill them with large flowers. For plant arrangements in zinc liners we tipped the front row of pots slightly forward to show all the flowers to advantage. These were in islands – for example, the pots were grouped round a big permanent lampstand – or they flanked a raised part where people had morning coffee and afternoon tea. We also put flowers at entrances to main restaurants.

We used mostly 48 (four-and-a-half inches) and 32 (six inches) pot sizes. Number 1s (approx. 20 inches) might be used for *Kentia* palms. We also had bay trees in pots. We'd trim and prune big plants left on board. Passengers used to tip beer into the pots.

Sometimes the lifts weren't working and it was hard, heavy work carrying a handbarrow filled with terracotta pots up narrow, semi-winding stairs between decks – and there were quite a few decks! The crew didn't help at all, except they ditched the spent flowers and cleaned vases afterwards. The prom deck was always well-decorated with flowers because it was a social area with lounges and smoking rooms.

We did some flowers for passengers but not a lot. The florists who did those were Fowler, Bailey's, Tomlinson, Sollis and Andrews, and ourselves in later years.

By 1964 you could see that everything was folding in the docks, which had been our main business. Father had retired by then and I went into the local authority working for the Parks Department at Eastleigh. Everything in Burgess Road is pulled down now.

On the evening of 26 May 1936 a special rail carriage brought an eight-feet-long model of the *Queen Mary* to the terminus station in Southampton. The base of the model was a wonder of wirework and its outer coating a mass of flowers. It had been made at A. Austin's florist's shop in Birmingham by the city's unit of the Florists' Telegraph Delivery Association and was to be presented the following day to the Commander of the *Queen Mary*, prior to her maiden voyage.

The fragrant model ship was taken from the station to the Southampton Gaslight and Coke Co. Ltd's showroom in Above Bar and illuminated until midnight. Police officers struggled to form crowds into an orderly queue to file past the showroom window.

It was all very good publicity for the flower trade and no doubt Birmingham florists, land-locked though they were, saw the *Queen Mary* as potential trade. The city was, after all, home to many wealthy industrialists and in those days it was only the rich who went on cruises. The trade they sought was 'bon voyage' orders for bouquets or arrangements, either to be executed by themselves and sent to the docks for delivery, or to be relayed, for commission, to a florist in the port from which the ship was to embark.

Although the Second World War brought a halt to cruises, once it had ended and liners were refitted, cruising began again, and the 1950s and 1960s were to be most prolific years for 'bon voyage' flowers. During that time it was not only the rich embarking on liners. London florist David Longman recalls his shop making up orders for people emigrating – particularly the '£10 Poms'

who left for Australia from the London docks. Longman's also had regular orders for passengers aboard Union Castle boats bound for South Africa from the port of Southampton. The boxed orders went to Waterloo to be put on the boat train which departed for Southampton at 10.35 a.m. every Thursday.

For port florists, trade was good. There was the carrying out of orders from other parts of the country and also home custom, which might include a large number of orders from local shipping agents. However, port floristry was not without its difficulties, particularly in the early days. Douglas Bailey, whose firm were port florists in Southampton for many years (in fact during the 1950s they had a shop in the Ocean Terminal of the docks), recalled in an article in 1967 that in the 1920s florists were not allowed passenger lists. This meant that they were unable to deliver direct to a cabin and had to search around on board for someone, usually a reluctant member of boat staff, to agree to accept the flowers. Also in the early days fifteen-shilling flower arrangements were delivered in sixpenny Woolworth vases and after leaving them on board a florist could not be certain that they would arrive at the passenger's cabin as they had been arranged in the flower shop work room. The invention of arrangement foundations like Florapak and later Oasis®, which held flowers firmly in place, helped to dispel this particular worry.

Below and previous page: Illustrations from a 1920s floristry magazine.

Even when passenger lists became available to them, florists could still encounter delivery problems. A bunch of 'bon voyage' flowers might be requested for a Mrs E. Brown on board a certain ship; however, that ship could have 2,000 passengers among which there might be several Mrs E. Browns, and it did not help that a ship of that size was like a small town that had sprung up overnight, with the inhabitants all strangers.

Ideal delivery instructions gave a prefix – Mr, Mrs, Miss, Dr, Col., etc. – and included the full Christian names of the customer, for even if their cabin number changed at the last moment their Christian names would not. Stage and screen personalities travelling under their proper names but having flowers sent to them in their stage name (and vice versa), and people asking for their names not to be put on a passenger list, were irritations it was difficult to do anything about.

Bob Fowler of Southampton did a lot of port floristry work and for one of the '*Queen*s' bound for the United States his staff might have as many as 300 or 400 orders to deliver. He explained how he planned ahead, for delivery time had to be worked out according to how many deliveries were to be made and the ship's sailing time:

If there was a new ship I'd go down to find out what the cabin numbering was – say, even numbers on one side and odd on the other. It differed in various ships. I'd make a plan of the ship so that when the girls went down to deliver they wouldn't spend time trying to find the different numbered cabins.

The German and French boats sailed late at night or even during the night. They only stayed in dock three hours because of dock fees. The Castle line boats left at 4.00 p.m. every Friday, most of the others between 11.00 a.m. and 2.00 p.m.

We had our own vans to go down to the dock, but when things got hectic off-duty ambulance drivers used to help us. Saturdays were busy: you could have some three or four ships leaving on that day and you'd have staff split according to sailing times, between opposite ends of the docks. That's when we could have used a mobile phone! The girls did try and use pay phones in the docks but there were often people waiting to use them.

CORONATION YEAR 1953

Have you friends from overseas visiting England this summer?

On arrival greet them with flowers at their hotel or apartment — the fragrance and beauty of a lovely floral gift will express to overseas visitors your warmest welcome.

We deliver anywhere in London, at any time, Sundays included.

And when they return let their last impression be a happy one. Our Bon Voyage flowers-to-cabin service at any port will ensure this. Say "*Au Revoir*" with flowers.

LONGMANS LTD.
Florists,
21 FENCHURCH STREET, E.C.3.
Telephones: MANsion House 3833/4 and 0247.

At your Service

Bob's daughter Diana, although having a career elsewhere, helped out when at home and was often one of the girls in the delivery team. She describes the exercise:

A Longman's leaflet from 1953, advertising their 'bon voyage' service of supplying flowers to the cabins of liners.

With practice you could manage to carry two boxes plus one either side on a string and in your hand an arrangement, with your thumb always at the back of it so that you didn't disturb the flowers. Some arrangements could be as heavy as five pounds. The girls would organize how they delivered – some did all on A deck, others B deck – and used to dash about.

If there was some doubt over a recipient – say they might have changed their cabin after the passenger list went out, or be a late booking – we used to try and check the name on the cabin door, or there might be a reservation with a name on it on a table or on a baggage label. That all took time, and if the door was locked we had to look for a steward.

Despite impediments, the deliveries to the ships used to be duly accomplished. In fact, Fowler's had a very good reputation for delivering against the odds. Bob explains how it all stemmed from something that happened in 1926, the year of the General Strike:

Above: In its early days, the Majestic *had a ship's gardener aboard. This is his plant house.*

The *Majestic* of the White Star line was due to sail at twelve noon but because of the strike most of the bedroom stewards remained alongside, not on board. However, the White Star secretary had another company of stewards at Portsmouth willing to work, so the line decided to sail the ship at eleven o'clock and pick the men up off Cowes. Father went down with what was the last few orders, one a Gainsborough basket and three or four boxes tied with string, but when he got to the quayside the ship was just moving away. There was a crane at the bow end which had just moved the gangplank away and the driver shouted to Father, 'I'm letting down the hook – put them on it!' Father put the basket on to the hook and also the string holding the boxes and the crane driver swung them on deck. Fortunately the local paper, the *Echo*, took a photo of this and we used it as an advert afterwards!

Ken Davis comes from an enterprising family background. His grandfather was a plasterer in Swindon but when he found that it was not paying and saw how the population of Swindon was rising, he decided to go into market gardening. He grew all vegetables and his son joined him in the business. After a while they found that they could not compete with the amount of vegetables being produced and sold by market gardeners from the Evesham area, so they decided to grow flowers too and also deal in fruit. They then relied on very local trade. By the time Ken joined the firm burgeoning industries in Swindon were paying high wages and it was difficult to get staff, so he decided to concentrate more on retailing than growing and from then on the shop sold flowers, china and glass.

Above: Ken Davis.

In the 1970s the business added another string to its operations. It became an agent/florist for A.C. Rentaplant, a firm owned by Alan Cornford, who had pioneered the idea of 'internal landscape'. On Rentaplant's behalf the company maintained plants in offices as far afield as Eastbourne. Then Mr Cornford asked if they would provide plants for the liner *Queen Elizabeth 2* (*QE2*). It was an opportunity to turn the firm's entrepreneurial flair to something unique, as Ken explains:

> With offices you can do the plants every three weeks and that's OK. But we'd do the plants on the *QE2* and if she was away a long time at sea the plants didn't survive without attention. Now the ship was staffed a bit like an American hotel with a hotel director and one onshore too. The onshore director in Southampton asked me about the cost of putting a gardener on board. I said, 'You want a flower shop not a gardener, plus a couple of girls to look after the plants. Find us a cupboard to work in as a trial and we'll do two trips. On the first the two girls will pay as passengers and if it's a disaster that'll be it but if it goes OK we could come to some arrangement for making it permanent.'
>
> This was agreed and a spot found for the shop. It was the only flower shop in a ship in the world!
>
> It's cheaper to buy flowers here than in America so on the *QE2's* New York run we'd stock up the flower shop and decorate the liner when she was in Southampton docks. She's big. I don't know whether you know Old Swindon, but it's virtually a square in the middle with Wood Street running up one side. Well, it was like having half of Wood Street tied up there to decorate, and at twelve o'clock all would be suddenly gone – she'd pull out dead on time, no warnings and you had to be off. If you failed and were taken off on a pilot boat you were fined, but that never happened to any of our staff. When we first started it used to be a two-day turn around but by the time we finished it had become only five hours.
>
> We'd put on nearly three-quarters of a ton in flowers alone, plants were extra. There could be eight people involved – five from Swindon and three on the ship – because if there was a lot of work to be done we used the girls who were coming off duty from work in the flower shop as well as those going on to take over.

I asked Ken if it was difficult to find girls willing to work on the boat.

> No, there was always a demand, but we had to insist they did it on shifts and also worked in our ordinary shops at Swindon, Marlborough and Newbury. I started off with two girls but in busy times there were three. I

used to say to them before they went on board, 'Just forget the world you live in – you'll move in classes you never dreamed of.' In the evenings they were hostesses for first-class passengers at the captain's table.

I used to plan out staff for a year. Sometimes I'd fly them home from Australia if they were going to be on board too long. It was a lot of hard work for them.

When I was interviewing Ken, one of his florists, Elaine Dent, who worked in the *QE2* flower shop from 1983 until 1986, joined us. She confirmed the hard work:

Southampton to New York was known as the Transatlantic and the journey took five days. During that time we had to serve in the shop and carry out customers' orders, and do compliments gifts – for example, flowers from travel agents to their first-class passengers – and also any Interflora orders coming from onshore. In addition to that we did all the restaurant vases and took it in turn each morning to go round and water and dust all the plants. We'd also do a flower-arranging demonstration, which was very popular. In between all that we had to make up to 300 or 400 corsages and buttonholes for the first-class passengers for a formal last-but-one-night dinner on board and prepare 371 cabin arrangements. These were for putting into the cabins when we docked at New York before the fresh passengers boarded for the return journey.

Since the ship was tiny, to store these arrangements Ken had some special trays made with holes cut into them. The trays were fixed on to steel poles, one beneath the other and each had cabin numbers on. The flower shop girls were allowed to store them just for a day by what the crew called the 'shell doors' of the hull. Elaine carried on:

Usually it took two people twelve or thirteen hours to make the arrangements but once I and another girl made them in six – it was a record! Of course we had to unlock 371 cabin doors to put each one in and you got a sore finger and thumb doing this.

I once did thirty days on the trot – that was three transatlantic crossings to New York and back – and I was so tired I couldn't think straight. We often worked from 6.00 a.m. until 1.00 a.m. The pressure of work wasn't helped by the fact that coming back with the time difference you'd lose an hour every night.

Caribbean cruises began in December and didn't return until April. The first port of call was New York; then there'd be a couple of Caribbean Christmas trips, followed by some New Year party cruises; and then we'd go off on a world cruise. Say three girls had been on at the beginning of December – once the Caribbean and party cruises were over in January one would fly home, probably from New York, and the other two stayed on until the end of April. You worked hard every day, still did 371 fresh cabin arrangements each week and the only time we shut the shop was when in port. I often didn't know the day of the week. Then I might hear the church bell and think, 'Oh, it's Sunday, better check the church arrangement' – the church was in fact the cinema, converted for the day.

I asked how they had managed to keep up stocks of fresh flowers for the shop during the long trips. Ken replied:

Three of Ken Davis's staff in their shop on board ship. Elaine Dent is on the right.

Start off with flowers here, then in New York pick up from Fellan's, a firm of wholesale florists. Then pick up at various ports. In all there were ninety-five different ports where we made arrangements to pick up flowers. The girls would telex an order from the boat to me in Swindon – the telex here was always rattling. I'd try and find an Interflora member who would supply direct or we'd use their wholesalers, and Cunard would facilitate dock entry.

You got to know regulars. For example, Miami and Los Angeles were good; New York wasn't so friendly – too big. In Hong Kong there was a mini-refit and the ship was in port for three days. Our flower supplier there, Mrs Lee, used to take our girls on sightseeing tours and be very hospitable.

It was exciting work for the girls but damned hard and terrifying. It was a thin line between exciting and frightening, for they'd have to look out for whoever I'd managed to arrange to be at the dock with the flowers and hope they would be there.

Elaine confirmed that things could go wrong. For example, the time in Bombay when the flowers they had ordered didn't turn up:

We sat for about two days waiting and panicking as time went by. We had to sail without them and so had five days with no flowers.

We used to have a basic flower order and some 'local' flowers. For example, we had anthuriums, the waxy flower, in Hawaii, because they were cheap there. Once there was a mix-up over the local flowers. In Brazil they brought on board crates and crates of some flowers I'd never seen before from the jungle. The bill was very big and we thought, 'Oh, goodness, whatever will Ken think?' We kept Ken informed of what went on by one of us writing a diary of what we'd done each day, which was telexed to him.

Ken recalled that amongst other obstacles that had to be overcome were currency restrictions, which affected their buying stock *en route*, and plant regulations. As he explained:

Strictly speaking you can't land anything because it's treated as being exported, so we had to get dispensation for taking plants off the ship and any dead material was dumped at sea.

If there was a strike at Southampton docks Cunard would fly Ken and his staff from Eastleigh airport to Cherbourg. They took the flowers with them on the plane and travelled by coach to Cherbourg and to service the ship. During the Falklands crisis the *QE2* was requisitioned and became a hospital ship and that brought Ken another set of problems:

> We had to take all the plants off, tons of them. It was lucky for us that Wills of Romsey, a well-known tomato grower, had part of its nursery free at the time so I rented that and took the plants there. But because of the length of time involved and the work it would need to look after them I decided a lot were not worth keeping so scrapped them and just kept the major stuff. When we went back I replaced the rest.
>
> Another time during a refit in Bremerhaven in Germany, there was no heating on board and a lot of the plants died. There wasn't much time to do anything about it and an additional handicap was that in Germany it's illegal to use commercial vehicles in the dock from Saturday lunchtime until Sunday morning. We flew out to meet the ship and got all the plants sent from Holland. As soon as the flower lorry was allowed into the docks, we put everything on board and set it out while we were on the way to Southampton to pick up passengers.

I asked Elaine how they had coped in the flower shop when there was a storm at sea.

> The worst I can remember is Hurricane Gloria. We were on a transatlantic run and had been at sea for two days. Battered grand pianos swept down the ballroom floors – they were supposed to be nailed down but they lurched free.
>
> If we knew the weather was going to be stormy we'd put all the vases away, jam the buckets together and wedge the crates on top of the cold store. I was never seasick, apart from my very first day on board, but of course other people were. We had some very big pot plants not far from the shop and fairly close to the men's toilets and when you saw someone go green you'd pray they'd make it into the toilets and not vomit into the plant pot.
>
> After a storm we'd tidy up and reorder and of course on a really bad crossing there weren't a lot of customers to serve!

I enquired if they had had any special or regular customers. Apart from a lady who always dressed in purple and always requested flowers in the same colour, Elaine couldn't recall any, but she said that generally on the Transatlantic run she'd preferred the English as customers as they were less brusque and demanding than Americans. She added:

> On the other hand, the Americans did dress up at night. We had to be smartly dressed because we mixed with the passengers and one night I forgot we were on the English bit of the Transatlantic and put on a huge silver ballgown with all my diamonds. As soon as I got into the ballroom I realized how out of place I looked because the English don't dress up. I felt terrible, but had it been Americans on board I would have fitted in.
>
> They were the best three years of my life. We worked hard but we partied hard. I loved the excitement, the crowds when we pulled into a port, all the hundreds of little ships which came out to look at you and meet you and people crowded on to the quay.
>
> I met my husband-to-be, Clive on the *QE2* and several of the girls in the flower shop also met their husbands or partners-to-be on board.

Elaine wearing her best silver ballgown.

Ken supported this: 'My daughter was one, she married an engineer who is now second engineer on board.' He also said:

> Myself, I never wanted to go on a cruise. Once or twice when the streamers went off and the band began to play and everyone was getting excited about starting the voyage and the anchor was being pulled up I'd thought, 'Well, I *could* stay on here . . .' But I was interviewed by the local paper not long after we started the shop and I said I wouldn't go on a cruise because it was like a floating prison. Sometime afterwards I had to go down to Southampton to talk to Mr Biggs the onshore hotel manager, and he had a glasstopped desk with all the sailing schedules under the glass and a cutting of my interview but he never remarked on it!

In September 1986, the shop closed. This was the result of Cunard's budgets for onboard floral decoration being tightened, and the shipping line starting to employ cleaners whose duties included looking after the plants.

However, in the mid-1990s, an American wholesale florist, Boat Blossums, which had been supplying flowers to liners for the previous ten years or so, set up a shop on the *QE2*. By this time the liner had changed hands to Carnival Lines.

The challenges of running a floating flower shop remain very much as they did in Ken Davis's pioneering days: for example, the problem of the short time before a voyage in which to get everything on board and in place; the difficulties which can arise in getting flowers aboard at various ports; and the tremendous effort needed to make up many cabin arrangements in a short space of time. As R. Lynn Hoffman, the owner of Boat Blossums, says: 'Working as an onboard florist is not an easy job by any means, but the rewards of travel are wonderful for the right person.'

The Queen Elizabeth, *one of the liners served by several Southampton florists.*

CHAPTER EIGHT

Funeral flowers

Up until the late 1920s–early 1930s it was usual for funeral flowers to be white and to this day there are some people who cannot see the smooth, waxy blooms of arum lilies without thinking of funerals. Gradually, however, and rather boldly, coloured spring flowers were added by some florists, who were, frankly, bored with all-white wreaths, and eventually coloured flowers became the norm.

The old custom for white may have been a legacy from the days when white flowers, symbolizing purity and virginity, were put on the graves of girls and maidens. But interestingly, early writings about the Christian custom of a wreath to signify 'purity of flesh and spirit' at the funeral of a child who had not 'reached the age of reason' refer to the wreath as being made out of aromatic herbs and evergreens; there is no mention of white flowers. It was not until medieval times that whiteness was associated with virginity at funerals – for example, in the ritual of a virgin crant (crown) at the funeral of a young unmarried person. The crown was made of fresh cut hazel and studded with white and black paper rosettes. It was suspended on a white stick carried between two young girls dressed all in white. Hung beneath the crown were five glove shapes cut from parchment. After the funeral the crown plus gloves would be placed in the church. It's thought that the gloves represented a challenge – a kind of 'throwing down of the gauntlet' – and that if after a certain time no one challenged the awarding of the crown then crown and gloves were hung permanently in the church and not touched until they rotted and fell. Shakespeare wrote of Ophelia being allowed her 'virgin crants' in Hamlet. The awarding of a virgin's crant took place as late as 1973 at a funeral in Abbotts Ann near Andover.

In the same play Shakespeare mentioned the custom of covering a corpse with flowers:

> White his shroud as the mountain snow . . .
> Larded all with sweet flowers;
> Which bewept to the grave did go
> With true-love showers.

In 1820 that exact description came to the mind of the writer Washington Irving. When, while in a remote part of Glamorganshire, he saw a corpse laid on a bed and covered in flowers. By that time this custom was sufficiently old-fashioned and rare for him to make a special note of it.

An Act of Parliament passed in 1849 was to have a bearing on funeral flowers. The Act made it compulsory for every town of a certain size to provide a cemetery beyond the municipal boundaries. This ruling came about because many town and city churchyards at the time were filled to the point that conditions in them were insanitary. In some, the digging of a fresh grave brought up human bones, which would then be left for dogs to scavenge. Many cemeteries were also dreary and neglected places. A contemporary observer wrote: 'I have seen some almost hidden with the gaunt, grimy walls of the great factories surrounding them, damp and dark rubbish-holes for the neighbouring houses with docks, nettles and other rank weeds hiding the mouldering records.'

St Martin's Burial Ground in London's Drury Lane. At one point the ground was so saturated with bodies the soil had to be raised to the level of the first-floor windows before more burials could take place. In 1849 it was described as a 'dangerous nuisance'.

The laying out of new cemeteries gave an opportunity to make burial places pleasant and orderly. Walks were made in them, beds of flowers planted and the whole looked after by a manager. In the early 1860s the same observer mentioned above was walking in 'the pretty cemetery of Ryde in the Isle of Wight' and noticed 'many graves decorated with cut flowers which were renewed continually'. He also saw 'a few wreaths of Immortelles' hung on monuments 'or lovingly laid upon the turf', which he noted as being a trend imported from France. Hundreds of similar memorial wreaths were placed on the railings around the Napoleon Column in Paris.

Indeed, France had a reputation for associating flowers with death. Up until the French Revolution the Church had only sanctioned flowers at the funerals of saints but in 1791 (a year after the Revolution had broken with the Roman church) when Voltaire's body was brought from Champagne to Paris, at every town through which it passed, wreaths of flowers were heaped on the hearse. The spot where the coffin rested on its first night in Paris was also carpeted with flowers. In 1803 the Institute of France offered a prize to the person who could give the best answer to the question 'What are the ceremonies to be used at funerals?' A large number of replies put 'flowers' at the top of their list. When Catholic worship was re-established at the restoration of Louis XVIII in 1814 the use of flowers at funerals faded but from the 1850s and the rule of Napoleon III the fashion gradually came back.

Meanwhile, in Britain, the Victorian preoccupation with funerals and mourning was getting under way. Books on etiquette gave advice on the correct dress and behaviour for such occasions; and in one, there is a tip saying that it was correct for wreaths of immortelles and wreaths of white flowers to be sent by relatives and friends to a house of mourning prior to the funeral. In large cities 'mourning establishments' opened. These were places of harmonious hush where black mantles, caps, crêpe collars, black streamers, bonnets, capes, coats and all sorts of gloves could be purchased, all under one roof, so sparing the bereaved from having to rush in an unseemly way to different shops.

With the building of new cemeteries not necessarily near a church, the journey from the funeral service to the cemetery was long enough for a cortège to provide an imposing spectacle, particularly if it was grand, as often cortèges were. Whiteley's, a large department store in Queen's Road, London, offered ten classes of funerals in descending order of grandness. Class 1 cost £37 10s 0d and included (*inter alia*) a funeral car with four horses and three improved carriages and pairs. Class 10, priced at £13 10s 0d, offered only a modern hearse plus a pair of horses. Naturally it added to the spectacle if the coffin, on view behind the hearse's glass side panels, had a fine display of wreaths on its lid; and wreaths secured to the top of the hearse and to the sides looked even better. Thus wreaths became the currency of show and even oneupmanship. In 1895 an article entitled 'The Use and Abuse of Flowers at Funerals' commented acidly:

Now it seems the moment death enters a house, one must run to the florist for wreaths and bouquets. Everyone, near relatives or simple acquaintances, is expected to pay the deceased a tribute of flowers. Vanity is coming in, everyone strives to surpass his neighbours by the size and costliness of his wreath taking care to attach a card which shall indicate the giver. The coffin is often hidden beneath the mass of flowers, tokens of so many varied sentiments.

Of course the popularity of wreaths brought good custom to florists and for many years wreath making was to be the 'bread and butter' of the trade. There was even a special wreath-making stand which Bob Fowler remembers his father using:

> They were like an inverted music stand with pointed ends on which the mossed frame was impaled. This top piece slotted into a tube screwed to the table and once it was in the tube you could turn the top piece to view the wreath whilst you were making it. There was no weight to lift and it kept the design clear of the mounted flowers standing on the table.

Funeral tributes were good business. Eric Treseder of Cardiff recalls: 'In the 1930s the wreath business was very large in the Welsh valleys. There was no florist there and we used to send wreaths in boxes by rail, four shillings deposit on the box.' Rosanne Hall, worked for an Aberdeen florist in the 1950s . She says: 'There was always plenty of work for the shop's driver through funeral delivery work.' Joan Jefferies of Turner's in Hammersmith Broadway, London, says: 'We still have the traditional wreath trade for the graves at Christmas and on All Soul's Day some of our customers (there's a fairly big Irish population locally and also a Polish community) follow the Catholic custom of putting flowers, mainly white ones, on their graves.'

Edith Richardson also remembers wreaths of the 1930s. Edith worked for Sarah Gaskin's flower shop in Grainger Arcade, Newcastle upon Tyne. She recalls:

> Miss Gaskin used to do a fair number of tributes for Co-operative Society arranged funerals. Wreaths then were priced at five shillings, seven shillings and sixpence, or more expensive. Some had to be sent by train. They'd be put in great boxes like hat boxes and taken to Central station to go to places like Haltwhistle. Others I used to deliver by hand. I could carry two big wired sprays and four wreaths.
>
> When I got to a house they'd often say, 'Come and have a look' and take me to the coffin. I found it scary, particularly as some of the deceased looked like skeletons and, of course, that terrifies you when you're a bairn, but they'd also give me a cup of tea and a piece of bread and butter and that was good. Sometimes I'd even get sixpence!

An invitation to 'look at the deceased' seems to have been a hazard of personal delivering, for Joan Saunders, who worked at the Cathedral Florist in Worcester in the 1930s, also recalls it. She would decline and get on her bike and pedal off at top speed!

Wreath frames were mainly sold to shops by florists' sundriesmen but occasionally if an out-of-the-ordinary shape had been requested by a customer or an extra large one was wanted, a florist might get it from a trader who made designs in wire on the spot in the large flower markets. Another source, if you were lucky enough to be near one, was a wireworks which specialized in wreath frames. Kathleen Bretherick who began her career in floristry in Leeds in the 1930s, remembers going many years ago to Douthwaite's wireworks when she wanted a particularly large harp frame. Douthwaite's employed a man called George, who, as Kathleen explains, 'was very clever; it didn't matter what you asked for, he could make it'. The wireworks was in Vicar Lane near the city centre and the premises incorporated a retail shop in a three-storey building. Arriving for her harp Kathleen was directed to go upstairs. There she was re-directed to the next floor, some distance above, and she eventually arrived at the correct floor. Laughingly she says: 'I never thought I'd have to go almost to heaven for a harp frame!'

The story of Douthwaite's is an interesting one. The firm started in 1883 and when Raymond Douthwaite, grandson of the founder, began work in Vicar Lane at the age of eighteen in 1932, the firm was making wire window and machine guards, funeral frames, wire netting, nails and fencing. Raymond recalls that trade

Raymond Douthwaite standing in front of his father's shop in the 1930s.

was bad at the time: 'Some afternoons no one came in.' He set off in his best suit as a salesman to secure orders. It wasn't an easy task but he was determined to succeed and eventually the business began to build up. He particularly enjoyed calling on florists' shops where he was greeted by young ladies and offered cups of tea.

The Second World War took him into the forces and rationing of materials made business at the wireworks difficult. After demob he set about improving trade by concentrating more and more on florists' sundries over and above the firm's wire-made ones. He went abroad looking for ideas and new products. In 1973 the wireworking section of the firm still continued but a new company devoted wholly to florists' sundries was set up. This was to grow to such an extent that larger premises were bought and in these today are rows of long shelves filled with dried flowers, grasses, scissors, paper of all kinds, maize pods, ostrich eggs, baskets of every shape and form, lotus pods, terracotta and metal pots, dishes and vases, bamboo – natural, painted or gilded, slim as a wand or thick as a small oak tree, tiaras – paper crimpers, candles – an Aladdin's cave of objects that the florists of times past could never have dreamed of.

Back to wreaths, Jean Ogilvie remembers the ones she made at her shop in Cork:

> People had never seen anything but round wreaths but we'd been taught to do sheaves. That's a stiff cardboard or wooden backing with moss tied on to it and flowers wired and mounted. The proportion of a sheaf is two-thirds at the one end and one-third at the other with a centre of slightly raised flowers, say, chrysanthemums. We did far more of those for the Church of Ireland; the rest of the community preferred round wreaths. A wreath was about thirty shillings – which was big money!

Making wreaths could be hard and exacting work. Bob Fowler remembers that as a small boy in his parents' Southampton shop in the early twentieth century he used to wire up tiny dried heads of gnaphalium and pass them to his parents so that they could make the 'strings' of harps or lyre-shaped tributes by twisting the gnaphalium wires on to wire covered in fine green thread. Occasionally artificial gnaphalium – with a little binding wire already on it – was used. Whatever sort was used, making the strings was a fiddly job and Bob says that he used to complain to his parents they were not using his offerings fast enough! He added that they showed the symbolic broken string that was usually part of such designs by preparing two strings and tipping one up above the other.

Opposite: This very large harp-shaped tribute made by Case Bros of Cardiff for the funeral of George V shows the traditional symbolic broken string very clearly.

Bob believes that an equally fiddly job was writing a name on a 'cushion' in flowers, perhaps in violets or little clumps of carnation petals. 'People were keen on names in flowers in days gone by. Now you can get foam bases for letters from sundries merchants.'

Rosanne Hall recalls:

We made wreaths the same day as the funeral because we wired the flowers and put them into a mossed frame and if they'd stood for some time they'd have deteriorated. Nowadays flowers on their natural stems are pushed into a damp base like Oasis® and can be kept overnight in a cold store. But every day was starting from fresh for us and you had to beat the clock all day! If there were several early funerals you came in early to do the wreaths. You weren't asked to do this, it was expected that you did, and we didn't get overtime. It took us years to get overtime, we fought for it. Florists are notoriously bad payers, and we fought to get lunch hours too.

Rosanne priced the wreaths she made but with one regular customer it was not a straightforward matter. 'There was a family of landed gentry, the Stuarts, who used to send in their own wreath base and flowers from their estate to be made up. It was often a puzzle to know what to charge them!'

On the subject of keeping wreath flowers fresh, Margaret Matheson, whose husband's family had been in business in Morpeth, Northumberland, since 1689 – first as tree nurserymen and then as nurserymen-cum-florists (the shop closed in 1972 when Margaret's husband died), says: 'Sometimes, instead of padding a wreath frame with moss we used wild rhubarb leaves, for they were good at keeping the moisture in.'

Joan Corles, who worked from the 1930s until her retirement with Birmingham city florists (the latter years with Margaret Tregonin's), pointed out that it was very important to get funeral flowers correct and that often people would stipulate what they wanted in a wreath. Being at a city centre florists, Joan's funeral work tended to be formal tributes like a laurel-leaved chaplet or a nice spray ordered by a firm. Family requests, however, might be more sentimental, such as the 'broken column'. Christine Hinds does 'columns' at her shop, Green's in Bermondsey, London.

We also do cushions and tributes like 'Rock of Ages', which is a cross on a plinth that is three-dimensional, with flowers all the way round, not flat.

A flower-decked hearse and coffin prepare to leave St Paul's church, Cheltenham, en route to the cemetery (c. 1900).

We might use double chrysanths for that because if you used anything smaller it would take ages. The chrysanths are about two inches across and English and sometimes in really short supply so you have to be up at the market very early to get them. Girls from college don't realize things like that. They'll say, 'Oh, can you get me some double gold chrysanths, five or six bunches for Friday?' and I say, 'One of the first rules of floristry is if you want anything get up at three o'clock and get it . . . sometimes you have to beg, steal and fight to get it!' We do names, say 'Grandad' in carnations. A lot of florists now use chrysanths for this but we still keep to the old-fashioned way, and do, say, 'Dad' in red and white. We also use lots of green, and no tacky ribbon unless people ask for it.

Christine's local undertaker, based at Rotherhithe, uses a horse-drawn hearse. 'He's the best; horses beautifully done, carriage bought from Ireland, a lot of brass trim on it, everything has to be just so and everyone behave properly. There are about two horse-drawn hearse funerals a week.'

Doing exactly what the customer wants in the way of a funeral tribute was one of the first lessons Prue Headey learnt. She describes making her very first shop wreath, after she had trained at Constance Spry's Flower School in London:

I was nineteen in 1956 and got a job as a junior Saturday girl in Dunstable. My first task was to make a one pound five shilling funeral wreath. I decided to do a foliage wreath of laurel leaves and sprayed them with olive oil and polished them and put a spray of flowers at the bottom. I worked hard. The wreath came back. The customer didn't like it. They wanted a wreath made from three rows of chrysanthemums. The old foreman at the nursery attached to the shop said to me, 'Come here, lass. I'll show you how to make a wreath for Dunstable.' Local customers did appreciate my London lightweight West-End style wedding bouquets, though and we built up quite a trade for those, but it took time for anything different in funeral work to be accepted. Thinking about the West End, I can remember one of the most impressive funeral tributes I ever saw was a cross in the window of Moyses Stevens shop in Victoria. It was made of individual hyacinth heads and the corners were amazingly squared off, just as if it had been made from masonry.

The architect of the cross which Prue saw was probably Joan Pearson; or it may have been Miss Fairbrother (later Mrs Slater), the senior florist who taught Joan after she joined Moyses Stevens in 1948 (and incidentally made Princess Anne's wedding bouquet in November 1973). Although Joan did a variety of work at the firm, she was to stay for the most part with creating funeral tributes and became famous for them. In the trade she is simply known as 'J.P.'

Order a wreath today and like most other florists' creations it will be made on a floral foam base – that is, the flower stalks will be pushed into and held firm by a dense manufactured material. A generation of young florists have used no other way of making wreaths. But to an older generation who were taught to make wreaths on wire frames padded with moss, and to carefully wire foliage and flower heads and secure them with wires to the frame, the advent of foam bases, for all their cleanliness and convenience and the speed with which they can be used, is, well, to be mourned.

Opposite: A splendid floral tribute made by Cypher's of Cheltenham.

Colin Woolley of Blackwood in Gwent, whose family have owned their flower shop since 1939, is quite forceful on the subject:

The foam base was the ruination of floristry. Girls go to a class for six months now, open a shop, arrange flowers in foam bases and think they can do floristry, but you need proper artistic experience to be a good florist. Not only that, but I could make a cross tribute on a mossed frame for two or three pounds and one made on a foam base would cost seven or eight pounds. Also, to this day I still feel you can't better moss for keeping flowers fresh. But of course today you can't go out and collect moss as you once could because it's a protected species. We use all foam bases now and have for a number of years.

Indeed, there is not a florist's shop in the land which does otherwise. So how did this phenomenal change begin?

It came from America. A man named Vernon Lewis Smithers had an independent testing laboratory for the tyre and battery industries in Akron, Ohio, which he had owned since the 1930s. In the 1950s the lab was carrying out some work for the Union Carbide Company but the company decided not to pursue the experiments. Another firm bought the moulds, equipment and lightweight crushable foam which had been made in the course of the experiments, in the hope of finding a use for the foam, but also abandoned the idea and Mr Smithers bought them. One day, considering a floral arrangement that he had purchased for his wife, he had the idea that if he could find a way of getting water into the foam it might become the basis of floral arrangements and work went ahead in the laboratory towards this end. Poul Einshoj, who is the managing director of Smithers Oasis® UK Ltd, takes up the story:

J. CYPHER & SONS
CHELTENHAM

It took some years to perfect the foam. At first it didn't absorb water easily. The way to get water into it was to build a tank and put two or three bricks of it in, then a bucket of water, then screw down the lid and use a hand pump to force pressure into the water. Also you could only soak it once and then it dried out very hard and it was difficult to rewet it.

It was decided to call the product Oasis® and it went on sale in America in 1953.

Of course, Mr Einshoj would not reveal the technical process for making Oasis®. However, he did offer the following:

Nowadays we use plastic for sockets and switches, but in the old days it was bakelite. Bakelite is in principle the same material as Oasis® – that is, high density close-celled material, say like bread you forgot to put yeast in. We put in an overdose of yeast, as it were, fluff the material up, blow it up to a light density, into an overall structure which will absorb water. Later on it's treated with a surface active material, a film of powder which helps build up its ability to soak up water. At one time it took ten minutes for a brick of Oasis® to soak up two litres; today it takes only twenty or fifty seconds, and we've made it less crumbly. We're improving it all the time, just as your new car will be an improvement on your old one.

Vernon Lewis Smithers, inventor of Oasis®.

So much for its manufacture; but how did Oasis® get to florists in Britain? In various ways. First of all around 1960 Raymond Douthwaite of Leeds went to America looking for new florists' sundries and in 1961 began importing some blocks from Ohio by sea mail. Meanwhile, a florist named Ib Ingshold had started to import Oasis® into Denmark but as freight costs were high, he got permission to produce it in Denmark with an American licence. Dudley Cocquerel of Cocquerel's Sundries in Covent Garden, London (he had marketed Florapak in 1949), got the agency to import Oasis® from Denmark to Britain. Other early importers were Douthwaite's, Smalley's of Nottingham and Floral Art Sundries of Southend-on-Sea.

Ken Rigeon, a salesman for Cocquerel's at the time, remarks: 'Oasis® as a base for wreaths was fairly slow in taking off; many florists preferred moss on a wire frame to a round of it.' Cardiff florist Cheryl Hopkins recalls that when she was teaching floristry in the 1970s, she was given some sample Oasis® wreath foundations in metal trays to try out with her students. On the early blocks for arrangements, she says: 'They were too heavy if wet and would fly away if dry!' Then Ken Rigeon says, 'Sprays came in for funerals and a small block of Oasis® was generally used for these.' By 1975 florists were starting to use Oasis® rings for wreaths and make favourable comparisons between the old and the new – it took forty minutes to make a wreath on a mossed frame and ten minutes on a foam ring!

In 1975 an enterprising company called James Naylor started business in a garage in Redditch. It began to make a variety of funeral tribute shapes in Oasis® floral foam. In the following few years the company's packs of hearts, cushions, pillows and crosses began to find a ready market. Mossed wreath foundations became a thing of the past.

Nowadays Oasis® has competitors, but with factories as far afield as China, Poland, Australia, Colombia, Brazil and elsewhere, and over 700 employees, it counts itself the leading producer of floral foam worldwide.

Vernon Smithers saw the beginnings of the success of his product. He died in 1973 aged eighty-three.

Joan Pearson, who has now retired, explains how funeral floristry had changed since her early days:

Wreaths *were* wreaths. Now florists just stick flowers in an Oasis®, all loose, nothing wired. We used to wire, even every ivy leaf.

It was hard work. For example, if you made a large cross, say five feet long, you had to chisel the wood yourself to make the two pieces, then you nailed them together. Next, it was mossed – that's putting moss on to it and wrapping it on with string. String wasn't easy to come by after the war but if you got it, it came in a large roll. We used an old sewing machine to make it into balls small enough to handle. I say sewing machine but it was really only part of one, a treadle beneath a metal frame which had a spindle on it. We pushed a wooden spool on to the spindle and wound the string on to that.

Before you used the moss you had to put it on to a plank of wood and tease out bits of grass, leaf or twig. The moss came in sacks from the market. It was bought by our buyer. I think a lot of it came from Wales. It would keep quite a long time but if it had dank water in it, it wouldn't keep so well and smelt horrible. You soaked the moss because wires won't go through it if it's dry.

Our wreath designs were known by letters of the alphabet. Each had the initial letter of the surname of someone who had been at Moyses' years ago and had set a certain style or liked to work with that sort of wreath. For example, Vs were chaplets, Ls were wreaths, and Fs and Ds were laurel wreaths in different sizes.

You weren't allowed to take flowers out of the shop for wreath making. You used instead 'OS' flowers – that's old stock – which were kept on a shelf. OS didn't mean faded flowers but those that were in stock for wreaths. Some flowers had no stalks, just heads, and these were used for solid bases (that's round wreaths, like a Polo mint with a hole in the middle), pillows and cushions. After you made a solid base you put a spray on the side of it.

So *many* wreaths were bought in those days. Often a customer would come in on the way to a funeral and buy a wreath off the peg, so to speak – that's one from a large blackboard in the window.

Sometimes people wanted articles made of flowers that were specific to the deceased, perhaps a hairdresser's comb and scissors. We used to try and dissuade them and advised having, say, a wooden or china item in a flower garden. You see, flowers made up to look like certain things are fine for the Jersey Battle of Flowers but on a small scale they look lumpy. Someone asked for clasped hands and really they looked like bunches of bananas. However, amongst other things, I've done big tops, TV sets, horses' heads, bulls' heads (you look at a photo for these) and the name Fulham Football Club in letters three to four feet tall!

The most interesting odd request was for a flower replica of a hopper used for recycling plastic, which had been invented by the deceased. I used white chrysanthemums to make it. Another time a customer had a coffin covered in grey felt and wanted the top decorated. I made a frame the shape of the coffin and put into it snowdrops, both stalks and heads, in groups, on moss and foliage, all over . . . it looked natural. I've done all red roses like that too and I remember on that occasion the client's address was House of Owls which is now open to the public. I've often thought I'd like to visit one day and tell them it was me!

Opposite, top: Members of the public crowd round to see George VI's funeral tributes displayed in the window of Moyses Stevens.

Opposite, below: Florists at Edward Goodyear's putting finishing touches to wreaths for the funeral of Queen Mary. The left-hand tribute of pink roses and lily of the valley is from the Prime Minister and the right-hand one of daffodils, arum lilies, cymbidium, orchids and roses is from the President of the USA.

One of Joan's most important tasks was a few years after she had started. It was in the early morning of 15 February 1952.

That was the day of the funeral of King George VI and I went with another person to Westminster Hall where the King was lying in state. The coffin was on a draped catafalque. The Queen Mother's wreath was on it and at the base the Queen's wreath and a few others, all of which we'd made. The King had been lying in state for three days and we went to refurbish the flowers in the wreaths. We were the only ones there and it felt awesome. In fact Moyses made, in all, 300 tributes for the funeral.

I remember, too, working on the wreath for King Hussein's wife. It was orchids – cymbidiums – and was flown to Jordan. When his mother died her wreath was to be laid out on hallowed ground in the desert so it had to be made of artificial flowers. When it went on to the plane the box was too big to go through the door and the box had to be made smaller.

Not all Joan's wreath work was for funerals: she designed many wreaths for other occasions.

When President Roosevelt's statue was unveiled in Grosvenor Square they wanted an arrangement and I did all pine cones. Then there were wreaths which President Nixon and Emperor Hirohito of Japan placed on the tomb of the Unknown Warrior in Westminster Abbey, and the representatives of the German Submarine Service wanted a tribute to the U-boat sailors lost at sea in World War Two to be placed on the bank of the River Thames. I made a six-feet-diameter laurel wreath for them decorated with a floral spray.

There were no end of wreaths for Trafalgar Day for Trafalgar Square, and a Primrose Day wreath each year for the Primrose League. We also did wreaths for the Cenotaph for Remembrance Sunday for various countries. The Ghanaian wreath was in green and white and other countries also had theirs in their national colours. Today most of the wreaths are all poppies, although I did notice at the last ceremony that one country still had its colours.

Two totally different commissions were for magazines. One was for an *Observer* colour supplement. It had an article about the damaging effect of acid rain and the *Observer* wanted a wreath for the cover and I made one of fir tree foliage. The other magazine was *Esquire*, which had a cover caption 'The End of Sex'. The magazine wanted a photo of a wreath to go beneath those words so I made one out of red roses but with heavily thorned wild rose tendrils!

Those were fun and you can keep the magazine covers as mementos, but making a wreath for a funeral is the last thing someone does for someone, so I think it's worth a lot of time and effort.'

When Queen Victoria died in February 1901 the number of wreaths sent was vast, and the size and complexity of the man- ufacture of many a matter for wonder. For example, the Institute of Journalists sent a seven-feet-high floral offering in the shape of a scroll with a quill pen at its base: and the words 'A Grateful Tribute' worked in coloured blossoms across the scroll. The wreath from President McKinley of the United States was eight-feet in diameter and its two- foot-wide band of flowers included lily of the valley, white roses, camellias and arum lilies. Interestingly, the widow of President Garfield also sent a wreath. It was of arum lilies and fern and was 'In grateful remembrance of the Queen's kindness to her'. No doubt this was a reference to Queen Victoria having sent a personal message to her at the time of her husband's demise (he had been shot whilst waiting for a train and died in September 1881) and a wreath of white roses, smilax and stephanotis for his coffin. Many of the grandest wreaths at Queen Victoria's funeral, particularly those from heads of countries, were made by florist Robert Green & Co. of Victoria, London.

On George V's death in 1936, J. Piper & Son, florists of Bayswater, London, took the opportunity to send a letter to prospective wreath senders. It is an interesting example of reverential respect for the occasion mixed with business acumen:

Dear Sir,

The 'passing out of the sight of man' of His Majesty King George V is a National calamity beyond the measure of words.

His Majesty's splendid devotion to duty, his beautiful home life, and his utter disregard of self, endeared him to all his subjects.

Should you wish to express your sympathy with beautiful flowers, we shall be pleased to place our services at your disposal and would send a representative with photographs of work entrusted to us on occasions of national bereavement during the last 50 years.

Yours obediently,

J. Piper & Son

The flowers sent for George VI's funeral in February 1952 were laid out on the grass outside St George's chapel. On the day before the funeral an eye witness wrote of a stream of florists vans coming ceaselessly through Windsor Castle gates, stopping briefly for details to be taken by the staff of the Castle Superintendent, then discharging their tributes before moving slowly away. The flowers sent were laid out on the grass outside St George's Chapel. Many were floral copies of the coats of arms of town councils and corporations, some seven feet high and so heavy that they were on bases of iron bars as sturdy as small bedsteads – but of course these bases were beautifully camouflaged. The following day *The Sphere* reported: 'As the mourners left the chapel after the funeral service the air was heavy with the scent of carnation and lily, rose and chrysanthemum, daffodil and tulip.'

Tram and bus services provided florists with convenient ways of getting wreaths delivered. For example, Bob Fowler recalls his father's use of the Southampton trams for funeral deliveries in the 1920s:

> Say there was a funeral in Bitterne Park – we put a wreath in a strong cardboard wreath box on the platform behind the driver. As well as using trams for deliveries we had two delivery boys and they often took funeral work on hand-pushed trucks. This went on until 1924 when father bought a two-seater car with an open dickey.

Transport aside, it was important that wreaths were delivered to the undertaker at the correct time. However, occasionally florists' customers are inaccurate over funeral times and it has not been unknown for a florist's delivery van to have to go in pursuit of the hearse. To avoid this happening many florists double check the funeral time with the funeral director. This is a small illustration of a happy relationship between two trades whose work comes together regularly and smoothly.

Opposite: Members of the public viewing tributes to George VI laid out on the grass outside St George's chapel.

However, over the years there have been a few niggles in the symbiosis. Take, for instance, wreath wires. When they were in general use, funeral directors disliked the ones which stuck out and jabbed the hands and ripped the coats of the wreath handlers. It was even worse if the wires scratched the paintwork of the hearse.

Lofty wreaths which do not fit easily on the coffin top while it is in the hearse can still be a problem.

Then there are the inadequacies of wreath labelling. A funeral director on a busy day might have seven or eight funerals and not be pleased to have a wreath delivered from a florist with vague verbal instructions and a message card which merely says: 'To a dear friend with love from Dolly.' Funeral directors put out pleas to florists to write a separate card or put on the back of the message tag the full name and address of the deceased and if possible, the time of the funeral. Also, in the days of many tributes per funeral it was helpful for them to have a note of the relationship between the wreath giver and the deceased, for feelings could be hurt if, for instance, a sister's wreath was placed in front of a daughter's on the coffin top. Legibility of tags was also important; a funeral director attempting to make a list of wreath givers would not be best pleased to find a pen and ink message washed away by rain.

Bouquets in cellophane bags, which became popular in the mid-1950s could also cause problems. These were known in the florists' trade as 'cellos'. Problem one to the funeral director was that the card inside could be difficult to read without opening the bag, and problem two arose because sometimes if the bag was opened the flowers fell out in a loose heap, as the bunch had just been put in loose and the stems tied over the cellophane. Cello bags had the disturbing tendency to blow up like balloons when the wind got into them as they were being transported on hearse tops and the undignified spectacle of one taking off and landing on a following car was not unknown. A cello-bagged tribute could also start to look a little bruised and worse for wear if after the funeral it had to be rehandled for delivery as a gift to the local hospital.

At the start of the 1960s it became fashionable to have funeral tributes as basket arrangements – the basket being metal lined and with a flat base. These were thought to be particularly suitable to be sent on as gifts for hospitals, although in general the idea of funeral flowers going on to hospitals seems to have never been particularly liked by florists, both aesthetically and in the days of wiring, on the grounds that wired flowers were difficult for nurses to deal with.

Of far greater concern to florists was an idea that was being mooted as early as the 1920s and was to worry them through the century. This was that flowers at funerals were ostentatious and a waste, and that the money spent on them was better given to charity. There was a certain amount of correspondence about this in *The Times*. The notion seemed to fizzle out but it never completely went away. By the 1940s, a survey of the *Telegraph* and *Times* obituary columns revealed its re-emergence, particularly for cremations, but comfortingly it was thought that

subscribers to these two newspapers were only one section of society and the lower middle and working classes would still buy funeral flowers if they could afford them.

However, in the 1950s, the 'No Flowers Please' issue seemed to be gaining momentum. A florist felt moved to write the following rallying cry to others in the trade: 'Neither florist nor funeral director can possibly afford to ignore the current trend towards utilitarian simplicity, both must work side by side, never letting an opportunity pass of combating "No Flowers by Request".'

During the 1960s, the funeral flower trade was still fairly buoyant. Derek Morgan, who had a florist's shop in Hastings at the time remembers that as late as 1968, he was still making thirty or forty wreaths per funeral. However, in 1970 a development occurred that was to fuel the 'No Flowers Please' trend. Rotary clubs started 'Flower Fund Homes'. This was a charity set up to build homes for elderly people, helped by donations in lieu of funeral flowers. Soon other charities followed suit.

By this time cremations were becoming increasingly popular, too. This affected florists, as crematoriums began to have their own displays of artificial flowers and florists were seldom asked to decorate them. Also people tended to buy sprays or arrangements of flowers instead of elaborate wreaths.

These trends, plus the decreasing size of families and the abandonment of old social customs such as a whole street clubbing together to pay for a wreath for one of their number, have seen the emphasis in florists' work turn from 'flowers for the dead' to 'flowers for the living' – that is, flowers for births, celebrations, gifts, etc.

However, as in all matters, there is usually an exception and amidst the decline of the florists' funeral trade one branch still blossoms – gypsy funerals.

Gypsies are very particular about flowers at funerals and the decoration of family graves with flowers. This preoccupation is apparent in cemeteries which serve areas where there is a significant gypsy population. An example is one of Darlington's cemeteries where there is a certain section which stands out. The graves are large, lavish, beautifully kept and always bright with flowers. Even the turf around the graves seems greener and more groomed than the rest of the cemetery. Most of the graves in this part of God's acre belong to gypsies. Likewise, gypsy funerals are generally big, and the more important the deceased was in their community, the larger the funeral.

Nattress's of Darlington has been making wreaths for gypsy funerals as part of its business for almost fifty years. Presently the firm is owned by Sally Bennett, but it was Sally's father Ronnie Nattress, helped by her mother, who started it. At first the firm grew and sold vegetables and flowers from glasshouses Ronnie had built

A typically well-kept gypsy grave.

on a plot of ground, and made the occasional wreath. If they were asked to do a large funeral order, where they needed a lot of flowers, they bought in extra from the local market. However, over the years they dropped the market garden side of the business and concentrated on floristry. Ronnie explains how they went about making funeral tributes:

> We'd start making wreaths a day before and be up to one or two o'clock in the morning doing it. We'd do an average of forty. There were no coolers then but we had three outbuildings on a north wall and they were really cool. I put the wreaths in them, covered in damp newspaper. In winter I had to make sure they were frostproof but if there was a very hard frost I had to redo some and replace flowers.

His wife describes the orders for gypsy wreaths:

> For gypsy funerals, Ronnie has done several mats of flowers, five feet by four feet, generally for the older generation of gypsies, and they always had the 'pearly gates' and liked harps and open books. A new thing is to ask for a box of rose petals, shoebox size, to sprinkle on the grave. We never seemed to do any large amounts for gypsy weddings, although anniversaries are marked, say, by a big basket of carnations and the anniversary of a baby's birth the same.

Sally explains the preferences expressed by gypsy customers:

They like wreaths. Sprays are not popular and preferred flowers are carnations and roses. The feeling is that carnations are more special than chrysanthemums.

Red and white flowers are liked and I usually do a five- or six-foot cross to go on the coffin alone from the family. This is a good solution to the problem which might arise over having separate family tributes on the coffin as there would be so many, so large, that it would be difficult to fit them on.

Sometimes we get asked to do big arrangements at the home of the deceased – perhaps one or two pedestals on wrought iron stands and flowers for a vase to be placed near the coffin, which is open for mourners to pay their respects.

On individual wreaths gypsy customers usually know what they want and each person wants a design that is different to the others. The 'broken heart' which has a zig-zag of red roses to symbolize the break, is popular. 'Cushions' and 'pillows' are liked and a 'teddy bear' is often given by children to grandparents. We've also been asked to do horseshoes, ponies and traps, lorries, lurchers, accordions and horses' heads. We build the base for these special tributes ourselves, sculpting it out of a block of Oasis®.

We've done seventy to a hundred tributes for one gypsy funeral and there would be more at the funeral, for obviously some mourners had used other florists. Many like to collect their wreaths rather than have them delivered but if we deliver, say to a caravan site, the men folk are quick to come forward and help unload. The wreaths are laid outside at first, and then the family ones are taken in. On the funeral day they're taken to the cemetery on flat-bedded lorries.

CHAPTER NINE

Flower shops in stores, hospitals and hotels

There are, of course, flower shops which are part of something bigger. In years gone by, grand department stores (more so in London than elsewhere) generally had a flower shop.

According to their 1914 catalogue, Whiteley's of Queen's Road, London, had a flower department and a staff of gardeners who would tackle any task from decorating a mantle or bazaar to laying out an alpine garden.

Harrods of Knightsbridge, London, has records which show that it was selling flowers in 1884, and probably earlier. The 1884 date is certain, for just after the store had been rebuilt following a fire, the *Chelsea Herald* of 30 August 1884, carried an article which described its new layout and said: 'Next on the right comes the fruit and flower department and here is to be a collection that will hold its own against any of the Covent Garden shops, while in flowers there are to be daily supplies of shrubs and blooming plants, nor are the beaux and belles' requirements in the shape of bouquets and "buttonholes" to be forgotten.'

London's famous department store, Harrods, was remodelled in the early part of the twentieth century and opened its beautiful floral hall in 1903.

Sebastian Wormell, associate archivist of Harrods, adds: 'When Harrods was rebuilt again, on a much grander scale, in the first decade of the twentieth century, the new Floral Hall built in 1903 was one of its most splendid interiors with superb tile decoration and plasterwork.' A 1905 store catalogue advertises that cut flowers and wreaths could be executed at the shortest notice and that buttonholes and sprays were on sale at the counter or could be made to order. There was also a collection of palms and plants on view. These were for table decoration or for hiring out to decorate balls and concerts. Harrods kept a special palm house at its depository at Barnes.

Round about 1925 the Floral Hall became the Confectionery Department and fruit and flowers moved to their present location in a neighbouring section. The flower shop is no longer run by Harrods staff and for some years has been part of Moyses Stevens' business.

Welwyn Department Store also had a flower shop. The store, the centre of Sir Ebenezer Howard's second garden city, had started off in 1921 as Welwyn Stores, selling food, household ironmongery and a few cut flowers. However, in 1929 when the store became a public company plans were made to improve it. The architect of Welwyn Garden City, Louis de Soissons, designed a massive red-brick neo-Georgian style building. When this opened in 1939 it was the largest store in Hertfordshire. It had eighty departments (with a conveyor system linking them so that merchandise could be quickly sent to the dispatch room), restaurants, open-air balconies and even a dairy for pasturizing milk and a bottling plant. There was also, situated near the main entrance, a flower shop.

Prue Headey worked at this flower shop in the 1960s and remembers:

The shop itself had two entrances – one was a door to the right of the main front of the store and the other was inside the store – and you descended to our shop via three or four large half-circle steps. We had a tier of shelves on which to display flowers in the store entrance lobby but a large plate glass window separated our shop from the lobby so we were away from the noise and bustle.

Prue soon discovered that being in-store the flower shop had a major disadvantage:

We didn't have a flower delivery van. We had to rely on the shop's main pantechnicon which took furniture, electrical goods and food. It delivered to certain villages on certain days. Our flowers had to be put on this with a docket but of course the delivery drivers weren't used to handling

flowers. On one occasion I sent a dozen white chrysanthemums which you'd only to knock and they would shatter. Because there was no one at home the driver pushed them through the letter box! I was in charge of the flower shop then and went to the store manager and insisted we had a small van to deliver the flowers. We got it and a driver.

Being shop manager also had its perks:

A grower of cattleyas and azaleas, Mr Moss, said one Christmas that he wanted to give me a present but I couldn't accept it at the store as it wasn't official and there was no paperwork with it, so he said he'd meet me at the station when I was going home. It was a huge azalea over two feet wide. I could just about hold it and sat clutching it on the train, for it was the old type of carriages where passengers sat facing each other and there was no room for it on the floor at our feet!

❀

The new Welwyn Garden City department store was built in 1939. The flower shop was to the right of the porticoed entrance.

Over the years, particularly when a store has been bought by a multiple, many flower shops within stores have closed. Hospital flower shops, on the other hand, are a newish phenomenon. A number are run by members of the League of Friends movement or simply a group of 'Friends' of a particular hospital. Voluntary work and fund raising for hospitals goes back to the days before the National Health Service was established when hospitals were reliant on charity money. For example, between the years 1897 and 1904, a charitable body called King Edward's Hospital Fund raised a total of £1.1 million which it distributed in yearly grants. In 1904 it held a dinner to gain money for a new operating theatre at Tottenham Hospital, London. On that occasion subscriptions and donations given by the great and the good who attended the dinner, raised over £4,000. Similarly, 'Society' ladies organized charitable events to raise money for hospitals. In 1910, for instance, Lady Juliet Duff held a Café Chantant in a grand London hotel in aid of Charing Cross Hospital, London. For the event she lined up a number of artistes including a ventriloquist, Russian dancers and the entertainer Harry Lauder (he, incidentally, had to cancel through illness).

After the National Health Service took over the funding of hospitals in 1948, some large hospitals had money in trusts, a legacy from the charity days. These trusts still run and provide finances for special events and occasions. In some cases this includes giving financial help to enterprises run by hospital Friends. For example, at St Mary's Hospital, Paddington, London, the Friends have a tea bar, a shop and a flower shop. Daphne Glyn of the Friends explains:

Irene Green of the Friends flower shop at St Mary's Hospital, Paddington, London.

Prior to 1960 our volunteers brought flowers in and put them round the hospital, then the shop started but in those days it was only in a porta-cabin. Now, however, the Trust money is required for more purposes because the NHS is so short of cash, so we have to run our tea bar, shop and flower shop as businesses as efficiently as possible. Each has a paid full-time manageress. I did manage to secure seven thousand pounds from the trustees for a fridge for the flower shop but that meant there would be no wastage and all our profits go towards buying hospital equipment.

Daphne explains how the Friends started at St Mary's:

They began about 1920. Prior to that there was a group called Volunteer Ladies who used to provide items like bed linen. They had a ball at the Dorchester to raise money.

My mother worked as a volunteer at the Middlesex during the war doing trolley runs, serving tea and coffee and doing shopping for patients. The Middlesex was financed by the Astor family. The head porter there wore a tail coat with gold braid on the shoulders. Constance Spry used to put an arrangement on the entrance table during the war – she gave it.

The flower shop is in a smart brick building with a plate glass window at the hospital main gate. There Daphne introduced me to Irene Green, the manageress. Irene comes to the job with plenty of experience, having spent thirty-one years in ordinary flower shops. I asked Irene how this shop compared to a High Street one. She replied: 'The main difference is that it's staffed by volunteers. I usually make the wreaths and bouquets but I am teaching some of the volunteers to do it. The flowers come, as to any normal flower shop, from a Dutch lorry once a week and plants come from a plant firm.' Daphne added:

The drawback to a hospital flower shop is that you can't advertise outside the hospital or put leaflets about it through doors. However, we undertake jobs like table arrangements for conferences at the College of Physicians and other colleges; and we do funerals, weddings, orders for nurses and of course flowers for ordinary customers coming into the shop. Also the hospital chapel flowers come from here and we give a special wreath every month for the service which is held for newborn babies who die – anyone who has had a bereavement can go to that service.

Mr and Mrs Fred Jefferies' (senior) hand-barrow, from which they sold flowers for many years outside Hammersmith Hospital in London.

Hospital flower shops not organized by Friends are run by commercial florists. The flower shop at Hammersmith Hospital, London, for example, is another bow to the string of the Jefferies family, who own Turner's flower shop at Hammersmith Broadway. Their connection with it lies with Fred Jefferies' parents. His wife Joan explains:

> Fred's father and mother had a barrow outside Hammersmith Hospital for many years. They'd buy in the morning, bunch them up and then be outside the hospital for visiting times. When Fred was a schoolboy he used to push the barrow round to the hospital in his school lunchtimes for his mother to sell flowers during the afternoon visiting and after school push it back again. The last visiting time was 8.00 p.m.

In the winter of 1962 it was bitterly cold and they made a little stand to go in the hospital hallway. Some people didn't agree with it but all the professors in the hospital said that they'd stood outside every night for so many years they should have a place inside and that's how the shop began.

Janice, one of Joan and Fred's daughters, showed me an article in a 1988 edition of the Hammersmith Hospital magazine about her grandmother, who had died that year aged eighty-six. The article stated how proud Mrs Jefferies had been of her shop in the hospital and added: 'Mrs Jefferies has her own unique place in the history of the hospital. She was known to everyone … staff, patients and visitors alike. It is hard to believe she has gone. She was a great lady and is deeply missed by us all.'

Up the road from Hammersmith a fairly new venture in hospital flower shops has begun. Simon Marshall and Ian Cartwright have built a smart conservatory-like shop within the gates of Queen Charlotte's Hospital and have been there since April 1998. They feel it is a pity that the hospital wall hides their shop from the road but have a signpost on the roadside indicating where it is.

Ian, who trained as a florist in Munich, was out on the day I called but Simon kindly talked about their shop:

Simon Marshall in the doorway of the smart flower shop at Queen Charlotte's Hospital.

We get our flowers from Covent Garden and a Dutchman calls with additional supplies on Tuesday afternoons. People think hospital flower shops are naff but we're not your typical hospital shop, not all carnations and chrysanthemums. A lot of clients have discovered us by coming to the hospital, say by going to ante-natal classes, and use us afterwards. We do some funeral work and recently did a big wedding at Fulham Palace.

I asked if being at a maternity hospital they needed a large stock of pink and blue flowers. Simon said they had a certain amount of those colours, adding, 'We've got blue iris in at the moment and pink orchids.'

On flower colours Joan Jefferies told me that years ago people did not like colours for hospital flowers and were particularly superstitious against red and white (blood and sheets). She said that she had even known a ward sister who *always* went and got a yellow flower to put in with any vase of flowers that were just red and white. I asked Simon if he had come across any similar hospital flower prejudices. He had not heard of the red and white one but said, 'Some people don't like all white because that's too like death flowers.'

Simon and Ian are young blood and enthusiastic but a number of older-generation florists feel that the hospital trade is not what it was. One said: 'People don't stay in hospital as long as they used to, especially in maternity. It used to be fourteen days before a mother was allowed out of bed, but now they can go home in a couple of days.' Another was thinking of giving up their flower shop near a maternity unit in a large Wiltshire hospital for the same reason, and also because: 'Security has got so tight that if the girl running the shop wants to go out and stretch her legs she has to phone to get back in!'

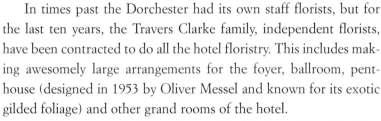

Hotel flower shops seem to be peculiar to London, and only the grandest of its hotels. The Dorchester, for example, has its flower workroom below stairs next to the housekeeper's room. If guests want flowers they simply ring 'the florist' or if they want something special and would like to discuss it they are escorted, in case they get lost among the labyrinth of rooms, down to the flower room.

In times past the Dorchester had its own staff florists, but for the last ten years, the Travers Clarke family, independent florists, have been contracted to do all the hotel floristry. This includes making awesomely large arrangements for the foyer, ballroom, penthouse (designed in 1953 by Oliver Messel and known for its exotic gilded foliage) and other grand rooms of the hotel.

The flower needs of the Savoy, Claridge's and the Berkeley hotels are all looked after by the Savoy Group florists. Their headquarters are at Claridge's and they have a flower shop to the left of reception. The shop keeps the name of Edward Goodyear, the previous illustrious resident florist. Ros Ackerley is a director of the present 'Edward Goodyear'. She has staff at flower workrooms in the Berkeley and the Savoy. Ros seems to keep long, hard hours and it is difficult to locate her to talk to her about the work – she is sometimes in the shop, sometimes amongst huge urns and pedestals in the workroom below, sometimes anywhere amid the hotel guest rooms or vast public ones. I met her briefly once, being careful not to step on a sea of table decorations which were being done by her colleagues.

Floral decorations at one of London's grand hotels, the Dorchester.

Claridge's seems to be a favourite for weddings and Ros found an album showing their floristry work at these. Most are 'Society' weddings which had been photographed for *Hello* magazine. I also learnt the intriguing fact that just prior to Royal Ascot race week the flower shop has to order a vast number of cornflowers. These are made up as buttonholes for the hotel staff to wear during Royal Ascot week and are also purchased by hotel guests who are going to the races. No one knows when or why this custom began. Its origins may lie in the fact that the cornflower is the emblem of the Coaching Club (founded in 1870) and club members and their guests wear cornflower buttonholes to their various meetings and events. During Royal Ascot week the club has always had a special place at the racecourse where they can park their horse-drawn coaches. The horses are led away for stabling, and club members and their guests sit aloft in the coaches and watch the races. It is likely that, over the years, both members and their guests have, through mingling with other racegoers, set a fashion for the cornflower to be the customary buttonhole for all during race week.

Five florists operate from the workroom at the Savoy. In the 1950s there were thirty, one of whom was Waynman Strike. His family had a chain of florist's shops in the north of England and Waynman had come to London, first to take a diploma course at Constance Spry's Flower School and then to get practical experience by working with top-class florists at various shops and the Savoy. Thinking back to his Savoy days Waynman writes:

> We had a workroom deep under the hotel. A normal day started with doing the large flower arrangements in the public rooms and restaurants before the guests were about. A lot of the middle of the day was spent arranging flowers that had been sent to guests by friends and delivering them to the rooms. This was when we made our all important tips. Then table arrangements and specials for the evening functions and finally just as most of us were about to go home we would get a long list of arrangements to deliver to VIP guests with the compliments of the management. We only saw guests when we delivered to their rooms or if we passed them in the hotel. We all worked long and hard.
>
> I think I got to the Savoy because the manageress there knew the teaching staff at the flower school. Without knowing the hotel management staff sex policy she thought a bit of muscle would be useful to move flower boxes and large arrangements. As my first name is Waynman the personnel department put 'Miss' Waynman Strike on my wage packet. It was only when I objected to the 'Miss' that they decided I must go.

Jackie Ferguson is one of the present-day Savoy florists. After leaving college she worked in several flower shops near her home in outer London. She then went to the Dorchester, where they told her, 'You'll either love hotel work or hate it.' She admits: 'I found I *did* like it and never went back to ordinary flower-shop work even though hotel work is twenty-four hours a day, seven days a week! Guests know that they can get a meal or a drink at anytime and of course think it's the same with flowers.'

Jackie explains the main differences between working in, say, a high-street flower shop and hotel floristry:

> The style of work in an ordinary shop is one-offs, usually bouquets or funeral sprays, but with us you do thirty or forty of everything at a time – say for a large banqueting room. Also there are two hundred guest rooms here and daily we do forty or more vases and deliver them to rooms.
>
> In an ordinary shop there are fewer flowers going through, but here we have a delivery of fresh ones every day. We often work in conditions which

Palms and floral table decorations at the Savoy, in London (c. 1920).

are colder, wetter and messier than shops. That's because we operate from the basement and do a lot of large pedestals, and the larger the arrangement the bigger the pile of wet foliage left over! It's also heavy work sometimes.

In the normal course of work we check the restaurant flowers daily and do the entrance flowers and other large display areas once or twice a week. Orders for decorating come through various offices like the banqueting office. We decorate for functions; the banqueting room; for small meetings or large conferences, and we do weddings and bar mitzvahs. Of course at Christmas time we do special decorations and have quite a number of Christmas trees. We're also a member of Interflora and have a delivery service.

A flamboyant mixture of high society and stage stars take supper in the early hours of a May morning in 1911, following a fancy dress ball at the Savoy. The tables are set in the hotel's foyer which has been lavishly decorated for the occasion with pink and red roses.

The Savoy archivist Susan Scott kindly looked out records of some of its early flower vendors for me. She explained that they had operated from a stall in the hotel courtyard, which has since been built on and is now the ballroom.

It seems that in 1890 the flower stall had constantly been under review, for in January of that year a Miss Arthur rented it for four months for £16 3s 4d (the yearly rent being £50); by June the rent had gone up to £52 a year; and come December, Edward Goodyear had taken it over and the rent was fixed at £150 a year!

Goodyear's vacated on 30 June the following year and Fuller & Co. rented the stall for 63s a week. Susan believes that after this the Savoy had its own company called Flora which bought flowers and fruit and vegetables for the hotel.

Society columns often reported on who was with whom at dinner at the Savoy and interestingly they frequently mentioned the table flowers. For example a cutting for December 1904 reports: 'At one table covered with Parma violets, the Countess Szapany was surrounded by friends. Mr and Mrs Sassoon were entertaining at a table decorated with scarlet geraniums and marguerites whilst Lord Lovat's dinner table was decorated with pink roses and lilies of the valley.'

The hotel's flowers were obviously a notable feature and Henry Pruger (hotel manager from 1903 to 1909) capitalized on this by holding themed 'flower dinners' on Sundays (Sunday was the 'smart' night at the hotel restaurant, the time to see and be seen). For one dinner entitled 'Springtime' all the tables were decorated with primroses and violets, and primroses and violets adorned the foyer. They also appeared on the menu and the sweets were served in sugar baskets 'cunningly fashioned' into, of course, primroses and violets.

Mr Pruger was known for his entrepreneurial flair and in 1905 he arranged a meal for which the decorations he employed, both floral and otherwise, have never been equalled.

On the afternoon of Thursday 29 June, George A. Kessler, an American millionaire whose money came from the champagne firm Moët et Chandon, decided to celebrate Edward VII's birthday on the following day with a dinner party. He went to Mr Pruger and said, 'I don't want an ordinary dinner. Can you do something startling – something that has never been done before?' This was a great challenge, for Kessler, who apparently was tall and dark with a pointed imperial beard and gold-rimmed eyeglasses, was noted for having hosted many 'eccentric dinners'. These had included a horseback one, where guests dressed as postillions and ate twenty courses on horseback served by waiters attired as grooms, and another in an egg-shell restaurant of giant size.

Mr Pruger, however, was to outshine all that had gone before. He had twenty-four hours, during which time he arranged for gondolas and Venetian scenery to be built and had gondolier costumes made for the waiters. Then he flooded the hotel courtyard, turned the water azure by adding washing blue, and put in and upon it live ducks, swans, gold fish, salmon trout and whitebait.

On the evening of 30 June Mr Kessler received his twenty-four guests in, as one reporter wrote: 'What was formerly the writing room and arcade of the courtyard but which had been made an ante-room whose archways and pillars glowed with pink flowers; pink roses were massed on the pillars, baskets of pink carnation and roses hung from the walls and banks of pink roses and hydrangeas crept up the walls, while the soft summer evening air, blowing over the water was loaded with scent.'

The guests then walked across a bridge into a huge flower-decked gondola and sat down on gold chairs at one long table. Four hundred Venetian lamps illuminated the scene while dainty dishes arrived via waiters who each had their own gondola. Musicians played in another gondola floating on the water nearby.

Beyond, round the walls, were hung pictures of Venetian scenes, including the Piazza of San Marco and the Campanile, and white pigeons flew about or nested among the flowers.

During the dinner a tiny elephant, loaned by the Royal Italian Circus, walked down the landing stage. On its back was a five-feet-high cake which, according to descriptions, was either 'studded all over with electric diamonds and revolving to produce a dazzling effect' or 'lighted with candles', or both. After dinner Signor Caruso sang to the guests from the musical gondola. The guests finally departed at 4.00 a.m.

Mr Kessler is reported as having said with 'supreme satisfaction': 'It was lovely, a dream of beauty … the prettiest, the most novel little party I have yet given.'

It cost £3,000 in all, and undoubtedly the flowers, which included 12,000 choice carnations, 2,000 Malmaison carnations, 17,000 roses, 2,500 cattleyas and 5,000 yards of smilax, had accounted for a sizeable chunk of this sum.

The gondola dinner at the Savoy hotel.

It seems that because of the magnitude of the floral decorations, outside decorating florists had been called in. It is believed they might have been a firm called Gerard, who up until the 1940s had a shop in Regent's Street.

There was one sad note to the whole occasion of the gondola dinner. Workmen clearing up on the Saturday morning found a dead duck and a dead goldfish, which had succumbed to the washing blue in the water.

The following week Mr Pruger turned the courtyard into a Japanese garden with lakes, flowers and waterfalls. Dinner for the Japanese Minister Viscount Hayashi and his guests, the Prince and Princess Arisugawa of Japan, was served on a table shaped like a large curved basket. Flowers covered its handle and were piled up inside. The sixty guests sat around its broad edges.

❋

CHAPTER TEN

Rising to the occasion

In the late 1950s, a family of florists in Huddersfield began to ease away from the conventional 'making-up' and delivery side of their trade and concentrate on selling good-quality, cut flowers at a low price. By 1961 the new side of the business had become so profitable that they decided to relinquish the old way of business and concentrate solely on selling cut flowers.

The secret of their success, apart from the lowest prices, was to have their shop in a busy shopping area and give it an open frontage, which encouraged impulse buying. Because the shop offered an already wrapped selection and flowers put into half dozens, it became at busy times practically self-service. On a spring day the number of customers often totalled between 2,000 and 3,000. Weekends were the busiest times, but in the early part of the week trade was boosted by flower club members and by students purchasing for their floristry courses at colleges.

In 1962, a report on the 'Market for Flowers' commissioned by the Horticultural Marketing Council concluded that there was, indeed, a large potential market for reasonably priced flowers; furthermore, that it could be served by 'flower-selling shops' which concentrated solely on cut flowers, with florists keeping the making-up and full service side of their trade separate from these new enterprises. However, there appears to have been no rush from florists to act on these findings. No doubt for most small florists it was difficult enough to keep one shop going, let alone two.

Interestingly, a similar situation had arisen in America ten years earlier. The first packaged flowers in an Ohio supermarket (placed there by an enterprising flower packager who was not having much luck with selling in local department stores, which were too hot and too expensive) had prompted the Ohio Florists' Association to discuss whether they should have independent outlets solely for cut flowers. One member had warned his colleagues: 'If the retail florist can't and won't take steps to meet today's situation then we must expect flowers to show up in supermarkets and similar channels of distribution.'

In the late 1960s, flowers were beginning to be sold in British supermarkets and then on garage forecourts. This development was the 'bunch trade'. It marked a split away from the retail shop type of bouquet for usually wholesale florists put the flowers together by rote, with no real finish and no high margins.

Opposite: Christmas has always been a busy time for florists. Holly wreaths for doors and formal decorations for interiors are still in demand.

Today's flower shops face stiff competition from supermarkets and garages.

There is the view that this method of selling, which makes it so easy to buy flowers, has raised awareness of flowers and helped make people who would not normally buy them do so. After all in a supermarket it is tempting to pop a bunch of spray carnations into the weekly shopping trolley. However, the traditional florist's shop, unable to compete with supermarket prices, has inevitably felt the draught from the competition. Similarly a growth in sales of flowers by post has not helped.

Bob Fowler, who has known the florists' shop trade for more years than most, sums up its future by saying: 'You've got to give super service.' He confirms that the strengths of florists are that they can provide designed, 'finished' articles, give a personal service and be able to deliver on a set day, but adds: 'I still think that florists need to be very much on the ball or else they will lose business.'

The main opportunities for florists to employ these strengths are of course special occasions. Times may have changed since the days remembered by Waynman Strike's father, of Stockton-on-Tees:

> . . . gentlemen customers phoning late in the morning to tell us they had just remembered it was their wife's birthday. Would we please deliver straight away as he was going home to lunch soon, and the flowers must be there first. Oh and could the driver say he was very sorry he was late *but the van had broken down!*

But nevertheless birthdays are still occasions for which many a customer prefers something more special from a florist to a supermarket bouquet. And there are many other special occasions for which florists' skills are required, of which Joe Austin's business meeting the floral requirements of exam time at Oxford University is but one example. Joe Austin's daughter Janet Carter explains:

> Around the end of May and through June it's exam time and the students come in for buttonholes to wear. From the first day both boys and girls wear white carnations; then on the penultimate day they change to a pink one and on the last day a red one. Sometimes they wear two different colours in one day.
>
> Also we decorate the dining room at Christ Church for gaudies – the reunions of old students and masters. There's usually one around 23 June or the Thursday of that week. For this they have a silver rose bowl on the top table filled with roses. The bowl is very old and valuable and when we used to fetch it someone from the college escorted it. Nowadays my son fills a container with roses and that's slipped inside the bowl at the college. What hasn't changed is the fact that they always want sweet peas in small oval bowls on the dining tables. It's been sweet peas for the last forty years and probably long before that.

No one at the college has been able to say how and why these flower customs came about.

The times when florists are very much 'on the ball' – and have been for many years – are Easter, Valentine's Day, Mothering Sunday and Christmas.

The Victorians set the fashion for church decoration at Easter. They thought lilies the most suitable flowers and particularly liked the trumpet lily, *Richardia aethiopica*, for both the altar and the font. It was considered that the classic simplicity of its foliage and flowers went well with church statuary and architectural detail. The love of the lily at Easter lingered on. Jim Segar recalls: 'You used to hope that arums would be ready for Easter and I had to consider the price. People would buy them and attach the name of a person who'd died and send them to the church.'

Welsh florists had their own special trade for the Easter season – specifically for Palm Sunday. For many years that day was called Flowering Sunday (Sul y Blodau) and it was traditional that on it graves should be clean and neat and dressed with flowers.

The *Cardiff Argus* for 21 March 1891 gives an indication of the importance of the custom:

There are few events in which Churchmen and Nonconformists join so thoroughly, and in which such an interest is taken as Flowering Sunday. Like other events, however, of a religious origin, the views of the people change and become more refined year by year, and a quarter of a century ago the Cardiff Cemetery on Palm Sunday presented a very different appearance to what it does now. Then, the graves were simply strewn with ordinary flowers, without order or design, and wreaths were few and far between, and seen only on the monuments and graves of the wealthy. Now, thanks to such florists as Mr Case, of Queen Street, the graves are strewn with flowers of the choicest and rarest kinds, and floral wreaths and crosses of beautiful artistic design are seen everywhere.

A visit to Mr Case's nursery grounds at Rumney would be a surprise and a treat to many of the inhabitants of Cardiff. The position of these grounds is excellent, and the southern slope enables Mr Case, with care, to bring to perfection and blossom some of the most beautiful plants of Italy and the South of France; and under the thousands of feet of glass he is equally successful in the cultivation of the still more rare, and more delicate plants of tropical climates, and thus, while years ago men of taste and wealth sent to London and Paris for wreaths and crosses for Flowering Sunday, the most exquisite designs, composed of the choicest and finest flowers, are produced here at less than one half the price formerly paid for them. Year by year, the taste for decoration improves, and on Flowering Sunday hundreds of wreaths and crosses, the handiwork of Mr Case's assistants, now decorate the graves of the wealthy and the middle classes, and the poorer inhabitants obtain their flowers from him and work out their own designs in the best manner they can.

During the 1920s a number of flower shops in South Wales used to advertise for small wild daffodils, perhaps to cater for their less well-to-do customers. Large amounts of these grew around the village of Dymock in Gloucestershire and local people picked them and dispatched them via post or rail to arrive at the florists' in good time for Palm Sunday.

Many Welsh florists refer to Palm Sunday simply as 'Palm'. For example, retired Cardiff florist Eric Treseder, recalls: 'Palm was the biggest thing in the whole florists' calendar. We used to work all night getting orders ready. Mother's Day drowned it in the end in Cardiff but in the valleys it's still buoyant.'

Valley florist Lawson Gwillim of Abercynon confirms that this was so. He says, 'About fifteen years ago I used to take two vans to Birmingham market and fill up. Now the Palm trade is not enough to merit my taking one.' But he helpfully suggested that he would ask his wholesaler when he called if he knew whether 'Palm' was still popular and if so where; and a few days later I received the heartening message that: 'Out in west Wales to Ammanford and past Llanelli it's still as big as Mothering Sunday!'

These days, when there is less emphasis on church decoration, Easter, on the whole, does not provide the trade it once did. Nevertheless there are still a lot of Easter weddings needing flowers and basket arrangements of polyanthus, and small bulb plants are popular. Also, of course, the fresh colours of flowers in season at Eastertime – bunched daffodils and tulips – are tempting to anyone wanting to brighten up their home.

The custom of buying flowers for Mothering Sunday is not as old as some might think. However, the name 'Mothering Sunday' goes back to medieval times when on the fourth Sunday in Lent inhabitants of hamlets served by chapels of ease were required to go with their local priests to worship at the mother church. When this obligation ceased at the Reformation the 'mother' ideal was transferred to domestic life and on mid-Lent Sunday sons and daughters working in not-too-distant parts made a point of returning home for a few hours to visit their mothers and take them little presents. With the coming of railways and motor cars visits home to parents could be much more frequent and the importance of Mothering Sunday waned.

Its revival was due to a woman living in Nottinghamshire. Her name was Constance Penswick Smith and she was the daughter of the vicar of Coddington near Newark. In 1913 Miss Penswick Smith founded the Mothering Sunday movement, which combined the themes of the 'mother church' and the 'mother at home'. It took the form of a special church service held on the traditional fourth Sunday in Lent. The first services were in her father's church at Coddington.

Clusters of colourful posies outside a flower shop the day before Mothering Sunday.

Eventually the Mothers' Union published a small service which was widely used around the Midlands and, later, beyond. In this, children and their parents came to church and the children promised to honour their mother and presented her with a small bunch of flowers. Then parents and children went into the churchyard and placed the flowers on family graves, so linking the service with parents 'gone before'.

Miss Penswick Smith died in 1938 but her work was carried on by her friend Miss Ellen Porter. Churches in the region would buy many small bunches of flowers for the service from their local florists.

Around 1934 a commercial aspect to Mothering Sunday began to get under way in the Midlands. Stationery shops put Mothering Sunday cards in their windows and confectioners made displays of chocolates and put up notices reminding people of the day. Flower growers, particularly in Nottinghamshire, timed their forcing season so as to produce the maximum possible amount of flowers for the day. By 1948 Mothering Sunday business had reached such a pitch that one Midlands florist handled over 2,000 local Mothering

Sunday orders and sent out 160 more as Interflora orders to other parts of the country. A Nottingham florist called it 'the biggest single flower day of the year'.

In other parts of Britain, however, Mothering Sunday had not become a day in the florists' calendar and, in fact, some florists considered it to be the second Sunday in May which was the American 'Mother's Day'. This confusion had come about because during the war American GIs, stationed in Britain, had asked florists to send orders for them on that day. In order to clear up all confusion it was agreed at a council meeting of Interflora members held in 1948 that the mid-Lent date which went back to the old religious Mothering Sunday be adopted and promoted to the public.

In 1950 there was a national advertising campaign and by 1951 Mothering Sunday flower sales had increased in nearly all parts of Britain. Mothering Sunday had become one of the two major flower festivals of the florist's year (the other was Christmas). However, its rise was not without problems. In 1951 the favourite Mothering Sunday posy for a child to buy for their mother was a bunch of violets. When the price of violets went up in Covent Garden by as much as 200 or 300 per cent and florists increased their prices to compensate for what they had paid, the national press protested against 'commercialization' of the day.

In 1955 there was an even greater outcry. A cold winter had hit spring flower growers in the West Country and the corresponding shortage of flowers sent prices up in the wholesale markets. This rise, plus the florists' own usual percentage, made flowers expensive and led the *Sunday Pictorial* to write about Mothering Sunday being a 'most disgusting racket'. The Queen, staying at the time with Lord Rupert Neville, proprietor of Uckfield House Nurseries in East Sussex, heard the local clergyman preach from the pulpit against the commercialism of Mothering Sunday.

Realizing that much was at stake, with Mothering Sunday being second only to Christmas in business terms, growers, wholesalers and retailers made a concentrated effort between them to try to keep prices pegged, and gradually things settled down.

In present-day Nottingham it seems that there is not the business for Mothering Sunday flowers that there was in the mid-twentieth century. One florist

Sunday March 28th...

Remember Mother

Say it with Flowers

A bouquet of fresh, un-travelled flowers can be delivered when and where you want, at home or abroad, through any florist member of . . .

INTERFLORA

The Flowers-by-wire Service

there told me that he sells more general gift flowers than Mothering Sunday ones. Another who recalls the churches buying bunches for children (they no longer do), thinks that there has been a decline in Mothering Sunday flowers over the past ten years. She believes that people now buy other gifts such as perfume. For her, Valentine's Day is busier. This also seems to be the trend for most parts of Britain, particularly with city florists. However, there are some who believe their Mothering Sunday trade is equal to Valentine's Day.

America's Mother's Day was started by Anna Jarvis. After the American Civil War Miss Jarvis's mother had tried to get 'Mother's Friendship Days' under way to heal the rifts caused by the war. Mrs Jarvis died in 1905 and in 1907 Miss Jarvis asked her mother's church in Grafton, West Virginia, to have a service to celebrate her mother's life. It took place on the second Sunday in May, the anniversary of her mother's death. Thereafter Miss Jarvis campaigned for the United States to adopt that day officially as Mother's Day. She was so successful that in 1914 President Woodrow Wilson made it the subject of a proclamation and the second Sunday in May became officially 'Mother's Day'.

The annual occasion became a great commercial success for growers and florists, and florists advertised it to the full. However, this turn of events was not what Miss Jarvis had intended and she conducted a bitter campaign against what she felt was gross commercialization of the day. Ironically, though, when in her last years she was living in greatly reduced circumstances, she was helped financially by a small pension from the American Florists' Telegraph Delivery Association.

There was a time when the only significance of Valentine's Day for florists was that they were advised to 'Plant your Renunculus on Valentine's Day' – that was about 1840, when florists were flower fanciers and growers. Today the retail florist, particularly if in a big city, is more likely to be advised to take vitamin tablets to give the required stamina to cope with the surge in sales which this one day brings.

Valentine's Day has long been celebrated. In 1537 Henry VIII established by Royal Charter that it should be 14 February and Samuel Pepys makes frequent mentions of it being celebrated on that day in the diaries that he wrote between 1660 and 1668. For example, in 1668:

Valentine's Day. Up, being called up by Mercer, who came to be my Valentine. I rose, and my wife, and were merry a little, I stayed to talk; and did give her a Guinny in gold for her Valentine's gift. There comes also my Cosen Roger Pepys betimes, and comes to my wife for her to be his Valentine, whose Valentine I was also, by agreement to be so to her every year; and this year I find it likely to cost 4 or 5 pound in a ring for her which she desire.

So Mrs Pepys got two Valentines – a guinea and a ring; but there was no mention of flowers. Pinpointing the date that they became popular Valentine currency is difficult. According to the *Best of Everything*, published in 1876, even sentimental Victorian ladies seemed to get only 'illuminated cards and sachets'. However, perhaps the flower-giving custom had commenced by Edwardian days or a little later, for among the archive papers from that time of the London florist Piper & Sons, lodged at the Royal Horticultural Society library, there is a scrapbook that contains a photograph of Piper's shop window crammed with floral hearts and a large Valentine's card.

It seems that this vogue was brief, for *The Modern Florist*, published in 1951, states: 'Although at one time it seemed as if St Valentine's Day was doomed to die, since the war there has been a bold revival of the tradition. Floral Valentines have returned to favour…' The renewed flame was fanned by the Flower Publicity Council, who in 1959 'gave special attention' to creating Valentine's Day as a flower festival. They did very well in terms of publicity, managing to get several features in newspapers and women's magazines and even a flower Valentine on BBC radio's *Woman's Hour*, which attracted nine million listeners. However, the flame must have dwindled again, for most florists today believe that Valentine's Day flowers never really got under way until the 1970s. Indeed an article written in 1976 in a flower trade journal makes a passing perplexed reference to the inexplicable 'recent substantial increase in Valentine sales'.

Interestingly, several florists say the trend started suddenly – quite out of the blue. Cheryl Hopkins of Cardiff is one:

Valentine's Day was nothing out of the ordinary until the 1970s. Then one Valentine's Day about 1973, our trade escalated in the afternoon. Later, I met Joan Case, another city florist, and she said, 'Whatever happened on Saturday? Pity trade wasn't like that every day!' A third florist's shop had closed as usual on that day because it was their normal half-day closing and they hadn't expected any trade out of the usual!

The most romantic flower seems, enduringly, to be a red rose. On Valentine's Day in 2000, Longman's, a London florists, sold 7,500 of them. David Longman says: 'On an average day we might sell 100, so you can see how the Valentine's Day demand is out of all proportion and,' he adds reflectively, 'to think that years ago you were lucky to get a red rose at all.' He meant the florist, not the final lucky recipients. The first real florists' red rose was 'Baccara', raised in 1954 by the French rose breeder Meilland. It was bright red with dark foliage and was also long stemmed and thornless. However, like the majority of 'improved' flowers, it had no scent; nor indeed does today's florists' favourite red rose, 'Red Berlin'. Only white roses seem to keep their scent consistently and this fact is bringing them back into popularity in general gift flowers, but for Valentine's Day, the red rose still holds sway.

Flower shops at Christmas are busy with customers wanting decorative wreaths, plants for gifts or a bunch of flowers to make their homes look nice for visitors. It is a different kind of business to other peak times for it is spread out over ten days or more.

Years ago the staples of Christmas trade were pot plants, chrysanthemums, holly wreaths (1920s and 1930s photographs show flower shop fronts covered in holly wreaths and crosses) and Christmas decorations.

On pot plants, seventy-year-old Terry Headey, nurseryman/florist remembers that, as his father did before him, he found it necessary to plan well ahead for Christmas:

> Cyclamen sown in May would flower at Christmas; so also would solanums grown from seed in frames in the summer and brought into heat. We also had *Azalea indica* from Belgium. The plants arrived in big baskets which you could use afterwards as dog baskets! They had been grown in peat and they came loose-wrapped and tied round the tops, fifty to a basket. They'd be in bud ready to put into heat and bring into flower.

Joan Pearson remembers pot plants being popular in her early days at Moyses Stevens in London's Victoria:

> We had a greenhouse at the rear of the shop, about ten to twelve feet wide and twice as long. At Christmas it was used as a store for azaleas. The buyer would get them and we went out to fetch them when we were making up

decorative bowls. That was the small azaleas – the larger ones, which could be as wide as two or three feet, were sold as single plants. Hundreds of cyclamen were also stored in the greenhouse and we had to go and fetch them when needed and bring them up a staircase into the shop.

A beautiful display of cyclamen being grown under glass for Christmas.

As some people now buy their Christmas pot plants from supermarkets the flower shop trade on these has eased.

Joan also had to go into the greenhouse to paint cones red for Christmas decorations. She says:

> We used to start making the decorations as early as August. We'd do a lot because in those days there weren't many luxuries around and they sold well. We'd have a whole windowful – all sorts of things in all sorts of colours, like pine twigs decorated with baubles or kissing rings with mistletoe attached to them. We also used to make our own holly garlands, which went on a twenty-foot wire right across the shop. That all stopped in the 1980s.

The nearer to Christmas it became, the more frenetic work was at Moyses Stevens. Joan continues:

> Two or three days before Christmas girls had to be at work at 6.00 or 7.00 a.m. and didn't leave until 10.00 p.m. so they were put up in local hotels. A lot of the work was unpacking the volume of flowers needed as well as getting orders out. Flowers arrived at the shop in individual, different-sized wooden boxes, not like today, when you get all the flowers in just one or two large cardboard boxes. A wooden boxful of daffodils practically broke your back – there'd be a pile of boxes as tall as yourself and you had to ask for help to lift them if you wanted one which was down the pile!
>
> We'd be so busy and then suddenly I'd think, 'Oh, I haven't done them' – a standing order, always for the night before Christmas Eve, of two 'pillows'. One was of lily of the valley and the other of violets. I don't know where they went, but I expect it was a private chapel.

Robin Wayne of Swansea also remembers the feeling of panic as Christmas Day approached: 'We'd get so short of flowers we'd go to the bin for discarded ones to see if any could be salvaged! We used to sell hundreds of holly wreaths, mostly for graves, but now if people buy a wreath, they want it for the door.'

This trend has made wreaths more elaborate than they were years ago. Today it is usual to find nuts, fruit and cinnamon sticks on them rather than a few sprigs of red berries. Traditional holly wreath making, however, still goes on. Gypsies make many to sell to shops and in Oxford Janet and Peter Carter, although retired from their florist's shop, still start on 1 December to make 500 holly wreaths at their home for their son Robyn to sell in the shop.

Holly wreath making is not kind to hands. Rosanne Hall remembers that when she was working for an Aberdeen florist and went out at night to dances, she had to wear gloves to cover her scratched hands. Retired Newcastle upon Tyne florist Edith Richardson says simply: 'You had no fingers at Christmas time from working on holly wreaths.' Edith, incidentally, remembers that part of her junior work in the 1930s was hand delivering Christmas trees!

Recording even earlier Christmastimes in Newcastle, present-day florist Katherine Sloan writes:

> Great-grandmother Ellen Costello supplied the Co-op stores on a sale-or-return basis with holly wreaths at Christmas. If there were no berries on the holly, she used to boil dried peas and dye them red to make the berries. She then employed girls known by the family to help wire all the holly and berries to make the wreaths and this was done in the front room of her house which was in the centre of Newcastle (North Street off Saville Row). These were made in hundreds. She also used to go to the country for a few months to Blanchlands where they had a small house to pick moss ready for the Christmas trade.
>
> My mother Ellen Johnson had a warehouse in the centre of Newcastle near the wholesale market. At Christmas time crates of mistletoe came from France which we had to separate into bunches for selling and holly would be bought by the wagon load by my mother to be bunched for the Christmas trade. She was really sharp at the buying. We'd also get beautiful white pom-pom chrysanthemum blooms called 'American Beauty' at Christmas. We still do – they come from Guernsey but they're available for only about two weeks of the year.

Of course, today, with so much imported material, chrysanthemums now share Christmas with a wide range of cut flowers, which are gaining in popularity over the pot plant.

What are today's other Christmas trends? I enquired this of Patrick Segar of Felton, Wills & Segar florists' in London's fashionable Canary Wharf. 'Basket arrangements,' he replied. 'Countrified-looking wicker ones with an Oasis® inside filled with flowers and mossed.'

Baskets? Well, then some things never change. Here's William Faust, retired sundriesman, writing in 1948: 'Before the 1914 war the practice was to present baskets of flowers by the Johnnies of those days to their favourite actresses, particularly round Christmas time – an enormous trade was done all over the United Kingdom. They were mostly of the tall, slender type.' The baskets presumably!

❁

Bibliography

BOOKS

Abbotts Ann in Hampshire, Pamela Ann King, G.E. King, 1992

An Encyclopaedia of Gardening, J.C. Louden, Longman, Rees, Orme, Brown, Green and Longman, 1834

Book of the Household, London Printing and Publishing Company, 1862

Cassells Household Guide, 1869

Commercial Gardening, John Weathers, The Gresham Publishing Company, 1913

Commercial Glasshouse Crops, Dr W.F. Bewley, C.B.E., DSc., W.M.H., Country Life Ltd, 1951

Domestic Floriculture, F.W. Burbridge, Blackwood and Sons, 1874

The Early Horticulturalists, Robert Webber, David and Charles, 1968

Early Nurserymen, John Harvey, Phillimore, 1974

The English Way of Death, Julian Litten, Hale, 1992

The Interflora Story 1923–1973, Geoffrey Lewis, Interflora (F.T.D.A.) British Unit Ltd, 1986

London Market Gardens, C.W. Shaw, 'Garden' office, 1880

Manners and Tone of Good Society, A Member of the Aristocracy, Frederick Warne and Co., *c.* 1875

Nottinghamshire Facts and Fiction, Briscoe Potter, Shepherd of Nottingham, 1876

Now Turned into Fair Garden Plots, J.G.L. Burnby, and A.E. Robinson, Edmonton Hundred Historical Society, 1983

Our Queen, Author of *Grace Darling*, Eld and Blackham, 1897

Retail Florist's Handbook, T.A. Price, F.R.H.S. (ed), C. Arthur Pearson Ltd, 1960

Root and Branch: A History of the Worshipful Company of Gardeners of London, Melvyn Barnes, The Worshipful Company of Gardeners, 1994

Seventy Years in Horticulture, Henry Benjamin May, The Cable Printing and Publishing Company, 1928

Shops and Companies of London, Henry Mayhew, Strand, 1865

The Shorter Pepys, Samuel Pepys, selected and edited by Robert Latham, Bell and Hyman Ltd, 1985

Sixty Blooming Years: My Life as a Florist, Kathleen Bretherick, NDSF, FSF, Kay Bee Enterprises, 1996

Tom's Weeds: The Rochford Nurseries, Mia Allan, Faber and Faber, 1970

Wedding Floristry, Lynda Owen, Hodder and Stoughton, 1994

JOURNALS, NEWSPAPERS, CATALOGUES, GUIDES AND PAMPHLETS

British Flower Industry Association 'The Journal', Coronation Souvenir edition, 1953; January 1967; and May 1970

British Interflora 'News', February, April and November 1952; August, October and November 1953; April, June and November 1955; and June 1967

Cheltenham Looker-on, 21 January 1899

Cheltenham Town Guide, 1900

Chester Illustrated, 1982

Commercial Flower Growing, H.V. Taylor, Ministry of Agriculture and Fisheries pamphlet 1946

The Cottage Gardener and Country Gentleman, 30 September 1852; 2 February 1858; 9 February 1858; and 16 March 1858

Country Life, April 1951; February 1952; and September 1958

Dublin, Cork and South of Ireland Literary, Commercial and Social Review, 1892

Florist and Landscape Gardener, 1949

Florists' Sundries Catalogues, G.H. Richards of London, 1901 and 1926

Focal Point (The Society of Floristry Journal), 1968 and 1974

The Garden, 11 January 1879; 4 December 1880; and November 1968

The Gardener, November 1867

The Gardeners' Chronicle and Agricultural Gazette, 2 July 1870

The Gardeners' Chronicle, 16 September 1933; 27 March 1943; 10 April 1943; 10 February 1951; 23 June 1951; 8 September 1951; and November 1951

Graphic, 6 February 1901

Illustrated London News, 15 September 1849; February 1952

Journal of Horticulture and Cottage Gardener, 25 June

1861; 17 March 1863; 27 June 1872; 28 November 1872; 3 May 1877; 10 May 1877; 21 June 1877; 25 October 1877; and 30 May 1878
Lincolnshire Historian, Volume 1, 1947–8
The Lincolnshire Magazine, Volume 2, 1932–4
Local Trades Review (Cheltenham), 1900
Midland and Suburban Horticulturalists, Various editions from 1840s and 1850s
Nurseryman and Seedsman, 25 August 1949

Say it With Flowers 'Bulletin', F.T.D.A. British Unit, October 1947; March and April 1948; May 1948; July 1948; December 1948; January 1949; March 1949; and April 1949
Southern Daily Echo, 27 May 1936
Southwell Diocesan Magazine, June 1938
Strand Magazine, Volume X, 1895
The Villa Gardener, June 1870
Where to Buy – Cheltenham Premier Shops, 1890

Picture credits

Archives of the Savoy Group pp. 201, 202–3 and 205
Blakemore, Linda p. 81
Carter, Janet p. 35
Case, Jonathan pp. (top) 30, 59, 90, 130, 131 and 173
Cheltenham Library Local Studies Collection pp. 32–3, 48 and 177
Cheltenham Art Gallery and Museum Service p. 175
Christie's Images, London, UK/Bridgeman Art Library p. 8
COI p. 53
Collingridge, John pp. 84 and 116
Community Information: Libraries p. 193
Company Archive, Harrods Limited p. 191
Constance Spry Limited, Farnham p. 65 and 66
Cypher, Ron p. 145
Davies, Jennifer pp. (bottom) 27, 47, (top) 50, 67, 83, 111, 117, 118, 129, (bottom) 158, 189, 194, 197, 208 and 212
Dent, Elaine pp. 161 and 164
The Dorchester p. 199
Douthwaite, Raymond p. 171
Fine Art Photographs, London p. 16
Fowler, Bob pp. 46 and 72
Goodyear, Derek pp. 149 and (bottom) 181
Graphic p. 183
Harrison, Jean p. 93
Hatton Gallery, University of Newcastle upon Tyne, UK/Bridgeman Art Library p. 11
Her Majesty Queen Elizabeth II, by kind permission p. 149
Hindes, Christine p. 76
The *Illustrated London News* Picture Library pp. 168 and 185

Interflora pp. 5, 150, 155, 156, 213, 214 and 215
Jefferies family p. 196
Joe Austin's p. 49
The John Henry Company, Michigan p. 88
Lady Lever Art Gallery, Port Sunlight, Merseyside, UK/Bridgeman Art Library pp. 122–3
Longman, David pp. 133, 139, 142 and 157
Mary Evans Picture Library pp. 14–15, 19, 21, 22, (bottom) 37, 38, 79, 108–9 and 211
Moyses Stevens p. 52 and 54–55
Museum of English Rural Life, Reading University p. 102
Newcastle Libraries and Information Services p.61
Oasis® p. 178
Pearson, Joan pp. 38 and (top) 181
The Royal Archives © Her Majesty Queen Elizabeth II pp. 135 and 136–7
Royal Horticultural Society, Lindley Library pp. 31, 43 and 69
Segar, Patrick pp. 26, (top) 27, 28, (bottom) 50, and (inset) 145
Sloan, Katharine p. 75
Society of Floristry p. 91
Southampton City Cultural Services p. 153
St Clement Danes church p. 78
Strike, Waynman p. 106
Tomlinson, Frank pp. 3, 10, 13, 44, 120, 143, 166, 187, 206 and 217
The Treseder family p. (bottom) 30
Tullie House Museum and Art Gallery, Courtesy of p. 125
Victoria and Albert Museum, London, UK/Bridgeman Art Library p. 198

Index

Illustrations are shown in **bold**. Publications are shown in *italic*.